Praise for *Play Nice But Win*

———————

"In this super-candid book filled with revealing stories, Michael Dell shows how his development as a person was tightly intertwined with building the company he founded in his college dorm room. It's a fast-paced tale of launching a public company, taking it private, and then taking it public again, all while wrestling with colorful characters such as Carl Icahn. Dell provides a wealth of business insights but also something more important: how curiosity and good values are essential to success both in life and in business. It's a lesson he learned from his strong parents and shares with his wife in the work of their foundation to give kids better opportunities. The result is a book that is exciting, insightful, and valuable."
—Walter Isaacson, bestselling author of *The Code Breaker*

"Michael Dell takes you into the real world of building and transforming an empire, vividly describing conversations and deals with key players so you see the whole picture. It's a great gift for those on a similar journey."
—Ray Dalio, founder of Bridgewater Associates and author of *Principles: Life and Work*

"*Play Nice But Win* is exactly right. Exceptional entrepreneurs like Michael Dell have changed the world under great pressure, but with great success. Michael tells you how to be successful and true to your values in this awe-inspiring narrative of what it takes."
—Eric Schmidt, cofounder of Schmidt Futures and former CEO and chairman of Google

"Michael Dell is the rare leader who set his company on a successful long-term direction by balancing innovative strategy with consistent values. In *Play Nice But Win*, he reminds us that courage and conviction are the key to transformative change in any organization."
—Indra Nooyi, former chairman and CEO of PepsiCo and author of *My Life in Full*

"Many people have great business ideas. Entrepreneurs see them through. That's the story of Michael Dell, whose book takes us on a riveting journey from the dorm room at the University of Texas to the boardroom of one of the world's largest tech companies. It's a tale of vision and perseverance every aspiring entrepreneur should read." —Sir Richard Branson

"This is Dell Direct. With insightful frankness and humor, Michael Dell tells his story, that of his iconic company and the grit required to compete in the ever-growing technology industry. This is a book for entrepreneurs, leaders, and dreamers."
—Satya Nadella, CEO of Microsoft

"Michael Dell's journey is part of the historic fabric of American business. His story of multiple transformations through the decades has insights for leaders at every stage, from entrepreneur to CEO."
—Howard Schultz, cofounder of the Schultz Family Foundation, former chairman and CEO of Starbucks

"With rare candor and insight, Michael shares his incredible journey as founder and CEO of one of the most iconic and admired tech companies. It's the unvarnished story of one of the world's greatest entrepreneurs, a visionary with unparalleled determination and a commitment to leading with compassion and integrity."

—Marc Benioff, chair and CEO of Salesforce

"As Michael Dell likes to say, life is about taking a punch, falling down, getting back up, and fighting again. *Play Nice But Win* is as much a story about resilience as it is about business. Michael is candid about the setbacks and challenges he's faced in his life and career. The lessons he's learned along the way are important for everyone who aspires to lead."

—Sheryl Sandberg, COO of Facebook and author of *Lean In* and *Option B*

"*Play Nice But Win* is an autobiographical thriller, and Michael Dell is the gangster protagonist—never looking for a fight, but relishing every brawl once he's in it. By outwitting tyrants, takeovers, and dead ends, Michael relentlessly protects, transforms, and expands the product he tinkered with as a teenager into the multinational company Dell is today. Michael consistently wins not by exposing loopholes but always by *making* advantage of the rules. *Play Nice But Win* is a magic trick, and one hell of a caped crusader coup."

—Matthew McConaughey, Academy Award winner,
bestselling author of *Greenlights*

"*Play Nice But Win* belongs on the list of great digital-age memoirs. The quietest of the entrepreneurs who created the modern computer business finally tells his story."

—Malcolm Gladwell, host of the podcast *Revisionist History*

"This is the saga of how one of the great founders of our time launched his company, grew it, got it back, and rejuvenated it. Michael Dell's entrepreneurial spirit is infectious, and his behind-the-scenes stories are full of important lessons about leadership, collaboration, competition, and innovation."

—Adam Grant, #1 *New York Times* bestselling author of *Think Again*
and host of the TED podcast *WorkLife*

"In his new book, *Play Nice But Win*, Michael Dell provides a powerful portrait of his life—the early years, the obstacles and challenges, the successes and triumphs. Thoughtful and revealing, it shares an inside look at what it takes to become a good leader—and more important, a good human being."   —Jamie Dimon, chairman and CEO of JPMorgan Chase

"This book is an incredible window into what it's like to be in a founder's shoes, and the difficult work of growing a company. Michael Dell is not only an innovator, but a leader, and in *Play Nice But Win* he shows what it really takes to build the future."

—Marc Andreessen, cofounder of Netscape and Andreessen Horowitz

"Michael walks you through every step of his journey, from starting a company in his college dorm to pulling off the largest all-tech acquisition in history. Anyone who's interested in business at any level can learn from the insights in this book."   —Bill Gates

PLAY NICE
BUT WIN

PLAY NICE

BUT WIN

A CEO's Journey
from Founder to Leader

Michael Dell

PORTFOLIO / PENGUIN

Portfolio / Penguin
An imprint of Penguin Random House LLC
penguinrandomhouse.com

Most Portfolio books are available at a discount when purchased in quantity for
sales promotions or corporate use. Special editions, which include personalized covers, excerpts,
and corporate imprints, can be created when purchased in large quantities. For more information,
please call (212) 572-2232 or e-mail specialmarkets@penguinrandomhouse.com. Your local
bookstore can also assist with discounted bulk purchases using the Penguin Random House
corporate Business-to-Business program. For assistance in locating
a participating retailer, e-mail B2B@penguinrandomhouse.com.

Insert photo credits: photo © Larry Kolvoord—USA Today Network, pg. 5;
photo by Mark Matson, pg. 10; photo by John Mireles, pg. 11 (top left);
photos courtesy of Brian Dorsey/Brian Dorsey Studios, pg. 11 (top right, bottom);
photo © Jay Janner—USA Today Network, pg. 13 (bottom); photograph by Stuart Isett/Fortune
Brainstorm Tech, pg. 14 (top); The historic paper on which Harry You and Egon drew the initial
plan for the tracking stock, courtesy of Egon Durban and Harry You, pg. 15;
all other photos courtesy of the author and Dell Technologies

Library of Congress Cataloging-in-Publication Data
Names: Dell, Michael, 1965– author.
Title: Play nice But win : a CEO's journey from founder to leader / Michael Dell.
Description: New York : Portfolio, [2021] |
Identifiers: LCCN 2021016697 (print) | LCCN 2021016698 (ebook) | ISBN 9780593087749
(hardcover) | ISBN 9780593087756 (ebook)
Subjects: LCSH: Leadership. | Chief executive officers. | Entrepreneurship.
Classification: LCC HD57.7 .D486 2021 (print) | LCC HD57.7 (ebook) | DDC 658.4/092—dc23
LC record available at https://lccn.loc.gov/2021016697
LC ebook record available at https://lccn.loc.gov/2021016698

Printed in the United States of America
1 3 5 7 9 10 8 6 4 2

BOOK DESIGN BY LUCIA BERNARD

Author's net proceeds from *Play Nice But Win* will go to the Michael & Susan Dell Foundation,
which is dedicated to changing the lives of children in urban poverty worldwide.

Four Seasons one night and thought I was doing a pretty good job maître d'-ing. They offered me a higher hourly rate, and I went for it.

I remember one time when I was working at Los Tios, a car drives up, and it's the immigration police. And all my colleagues vanished like that—ran out the back door as fast as you could imagine, and I'm the only one left. So these guys walk in, and I'm like, "Good afternoon, gentlemen. Can I get you a table?"

"No, we want to see who works here," they say. Very serious.

"Well, right now I'm the only one working here," I told them.

They stared at me. "Really? You're the only one who works here?" One of them went to look in the back. Nothing.

"Yes, just me," I said. "What can I get you?" Mind you, I was twelve years old.

My clothes would carry home pungent odors from my restaurant jobs. Sometimes my mom would make me strip off my outer garments in the driveway so she could hose me off before I was allowed to enter the house.

I also got a job at a coin and jewelry store, negotiating prices on gold coins that people bought and sold: the owner would give me a cut of each transaction. And I didn't just collect stamps, I sold them, at the stamp auctions I attended often as a kid—attended often until I realized that the auctioneers were taking a percentage of the proceeds. Why not (I thought) eliminate the middleman? I talked some of my friends into giving me their stamps on consignment, then, on a typewriter, I one-finger-typed a twelve-page catalogue listing their stamps and mine. Then I bought an ad in *Linn's Stamp News* advertising "Dell's Stamps," and mailed off xeroxed catalogues to everyone that responded. Sold a bunch of stamps, made pretty good money.

So I was sitting on some funds. And, all the while, begging and pleading and cajoling until my parents finally gave in. For my fourteenth birthday I was allowed to take almost thirteen hundred dollars of my hard-earned savings out of the bank and order an Apple II. I was beside myself with excitement waiting for it to arrive—days felt like weeks. Then one day I got a call from UPS saying the computer had arrived, but for some reason it was held up at the local warehouse. Delivery would take a while longer, nobody was saying how long. That was unacceptable. I made my father drive me over there to pick it up. When we got back home, the car had barely stopped moving in our driveway when I jumped out, carrying the precious cargo carefully, took it to my bedroom, unboxed the beautiful computer—it even smelled beautiful—and immediately took it apart to see how it worked.

My parents were horrified. And furious. But (I thought but didn't say) how could you understand it if you didn't take it apart? Assembled or disassembled, the Apple II was a beautiful thing. And one of the beautiful things about it was its open architecture: every circuit was on its own unique chip, so you could go in and start to play with these circuits and modify them. You could reprogram the BIOS (the Basic Input/Output System: the program, embedded on a chip on the motherboard, that controlled all the other devices inside the computer) and upgrade it.

This is amazing, I thought. *I can program my own computer.*

There was more. Back before the internet, before CompuServe or Prodigy or AOL, there used to be something called the Computerized Bulletin Board System (CBBS): using a Hayes modem (a brand-new invention at the time), you could dial in and communicate with people all around the country—learn and socialize and play games. That seemed super intriguing to me, so I bought a modem and set up a bulletin board of my own. But of course it wouldn't do if my mom or dad picked up the phone and heard modem tones instead of a dial tone, so it made perfect sense to me to call Southwestern Bell and ask them to come and install another phone line in the house.

Luckily for me, my parents were more amused than angry.

Word got around that I knew a thing or two about computers. I soon began tutoring kids in the neighborhood on how to get the most out of their Apple IIs. That became a pretty lucrative sideline. I also joined HAAUG, the Houston-Area Apple User Group—hundreds of techies getting together once or twice a month at a local library to talk upgrades and trade parts and swap stories. I would hang out with these guys (they were almost all guys) and get all kinds of ideas about how to modify my Apple II. HAAUG also sent out a dot-matrix-printed monthly newsletter, containing important information like the following:

> One of the least expensive (and thus surprisingly underpublicized) accessories for the APPLE II is the Programmer's Aid #1. The PA#1 is a single 2K-byte ROM chip which plugs into socket D0 of your APPLE. It contains a "library" of routines which integer BASIC users frequently need but don't always have easy access to. . . .

I was totally into all of it. At the group meetings I met a computer engineer in his twenties or thirties, a really smart technical guy. I thought, *OK, I'm going to hang around this guy and see what I can learn.*

And together we came up with something pretty cool.

At the time, developers were writing software for the Apple II, and the problem was that they'd sell one copy of the software, then everybody would copy it, and the developers would never make any money. All you needed was two floppy-disk drives: you'd put the software in one and a blank disk in the other, then type in a "copy" command. Educators were some of the worst offenders—they felt like, "Well, we're educators, so we shouldn't really have to pay for software."

So my engineer buddy and I invented a copy-protecting method. Every floppy disk had a certain number of tracks—I believe it was thirty-five. We figured out a way of programming the software so that it would write some data on a half-track, in between the tracks: when you ran the copy program, it would copy the data that was on the tracks, but not the half-tracks. Result: no copy. We went and sold this to a bunch of companies that were writing education software. It became a little business for a while, and we did all right.

Then I read that Steve Jobs was coming to Houston to speak to our user group.

It was the spring of 1980. Jobs fascinated me, not just as a computer pioneer but as an entrepreneur: I'd read about him in the business magazines, with the same intense admiration that drew me to the stories of Fred Smith and Charles Schwab, Ted Turner and William McGowan. Like those men, Jobs had started with little but an idea and an intense drive to bring that idea to fruition. And like them, he was succeeding in changing American business. Jobs was just twenty-five, and the company he'd founded with Wozniak seemed poised to go into orbit in 1980, on the cusp of its initial public offering and the introduction of the Apple III, which promised to be to the Apple II what the Apple II had been to the Apple I.

And Jobs in person was even more compelling than he was in print. When he entered the room at our meeting, it was as though the waters parted. He spoke with passion about how the personal computer—*his* personal computer—was revolutionizing the world. He spoke in soaring metaphors: "It's now possible, for the capital investment of a passenger train, to buy one thousand Volkswagens," he said. "The difference is that those thousand people have the freedom to go where, when, how, and with whom they want to go." With personal computers, he was saying—with *his* personal computers—people would have the capacity to accomplish the unimaginable.

I was fifteen and riveted. I couldn't have begun to imagine that in five years Jobs and I would be not only colleagues but friends.

My family's move from Grape Street to a fancier house in the Memorial neighborhood coincided with the beginning of my first year in high school. As you might imagine, an upscale school district would have a really nice high school, and Memorial High School didn't disappoint. It even had a computer lab, highly unusual at the time. Naturally I took a computer class. Mr. Haynes was the teacher.

Mr. Haynes was teaching us about programming—a subject about which I already knew quite a bit. And at that point in my adolescence, I wasn't shy about showing off my knowledge. The truth is, I was a bit of a smart-ass.

One day Mr. Haynes told the class, with some excitement, that he was going to write a program to create a sine wave using BASIC programming language and that we could all watch him and learn. Well, that wasn't news to me: I'd already learned how to program in machine language, which is like talking directly to the microprocessor and is a pretty complicated process. It was not an easy thing to do (I can't do it anymore), and I was proud that I had mastered it.

And so the moment after Mr. Haynes told the class of his plan, I spoke right up. There was a much better way than BASIC programming language to create a sine wave, I said. You could do it in machine language, I said, and it would be much faster.

Mr. Haynes shot me a dirty look. "Okay," he said. "Why don't you write it in machine language and I'll write it in BASIC, and we'll come back next Tuesday and we'll see whose is faster."

We came back the next Tuesday, and he ran his program. *DIT-DIT-DIT. DIT-DIT-DIT. DIT-DIT-DIT. DIT-DIT-DIT.* Sine wave.

Then I ran mine. *VROOP*—sine wave.

From that day forward, Mr. Haynes hated me. And I'm sorry to say that I didn't mind.

On August 12, 1981, IBM introduced its PC, the 5150, a flat beige-and-gray box with a boxy beige-and-gray display on top. It weighed in at a svelte 25 pounds and had a 4.77-MHz Intel 8088 CPU that contained

29,000 transistors. Stripped, the PC had just 16 kB of RAM and no data storage drive: the bare-bones model would set you back a mere $1,565 (about $3,900 today). If you opted for the standard version, with 64 kB of RAM (expandable to 256 kB) and a couple of 5.25-inch floppy drives, the price jumped to $2,880 ($7,150 today). Available software included the VisiCalc spreadsheet; a word-processing program, EasyWriter 1.0; and Adventure, the first game developed by a scrappy little outfit out in Redmond, Washington—a mere six years old at the time—by the name of Microsoft.

Yes, the Apple II had lots of games, but the 5150 was not only more powerful than Apple's machine but more serious. IBM's entry into the personal computer market was a big, big deal. For years, Big Blue had a dominance in the technology field unmatched by any other company; during the 1980s, IBM was by far the most successful and valuable company in the US. And the 5150's software was tailored specifically to business users, of whom, it turned out, there were a lot out there. As *Wired* magazine later wrote, Big Blue's entry into the personal computer market would "effectively sweep away the competition and effectively have the field to itself, for a while." (Mark those last three words.) IBM retailed the 5150 through ComputerLand and Sears, Roebuck; it sold sixty-five thousand PCs in four months, with a hundred thousand orders taken by Christmas. And with all due respect to the riveting Steve Jobs, one of those sales was to me. On August 12, 1981.

I became an instant IBM convert. The personal computer as business machine (*business machine*, after all, was two-thirds of IBM's name) was, I believed, the wave of the future. As soon as I took my 5150 apart—which of course I did immediately—I discovered a couple of striking things. First of all, as with the Apple II, the 5150s architecture was open: you could literally understand what every chip was doing.

The other thing I found when I disassembled the IBM-PC was that there was nothing inside from IBM! It was all parts from other companies. There was that CPU from Intel, and every chip was marked with the name of its manufacturer. I could just walk into RadioShack or another local electronics store and buy the chips I needed. And the PC's operating system, MS-DOS, was developed not by IBM but by that scrappy little outfit Microsoft.

There was just one exception to this odd made-by-others theme, only one thing that was unique to this machine: the basic input/output system. The BIOS. But all that outsourcing was very strange, I thought. It would later become apparent that IBM had created the PC quickly and with off-the-shelf components out of expediency, because they were secretly worried about Apple's inroads into the consumer and education markets. So instead of creating their own operating system, which they certainly knew how to do, and creating their own microprocessor, which they certainly knew how to do, they chose DOS from Microsoft and the Intel-8088. They were such a huge and powerful company, such an American institution, so completely synonymous with the word "computer," that I don't think they thought anyone would ever challenge them.

The summer between my sophomore and junior years at Memorial High was an eventful one, and not just because of the PC. For one thing, I now had my driver's license, which expanded my horizons dramatically. I was used to riding my bicycle all over Houston to go to stamp stores or my various jobs or Apple User Group meetings—sometimes I'd pedal twenty or thirty miles, clear across to the other side of town. But that got tiring, and sometimes it rained. Now I could really go places: my father let me use the old family station wagon, a massive, light-blue 1975 Oldsmobile Cutlass. "If you hit anything, you'll probably be okay," my dad said. "This thing is a tank."

Driving also expanded my economic opportunities dramatically. That summer I got a new job: along with hundreds of other teenagers, I sold subscriptions to the (now-defunct) *Houston Post*, calling random people on the phone and trying to talk them into getting the paper. Being naturally ambitious, I wanted to sell as many subscriptions as possible. And almost immediately, I observed three things: first, that if you sounded like the people you were trying to sell a subscription to, they were much more likely to buy from you. I would talk to my prospects with a heavy Texas accent, strike up a conversation. Results often followed.

The second thing I noticed was that people who were moving into a new residence were more likely to subscribe to the paper. And the third thing I observed, kind of a corollary of the second, was that people who were getting married were much more likely to buy a subscription— maybe out of some kind of excitement at settling down and beginning grown-up life.

The beginning of a plan occurred to me.

In Texas, when you want to get a marriage license you have to go to the county courthouse to apply, giving the address you want the license sent to. And I figured out that under the Freedom of Information Act (FOIA), I, as a fellow Texas citizen, was entitled to go to any county courthouse in the state and say, "I want to see all the marriage license applications you received during the past year." I clearly remember the first time I did it, at the Harris County courthouse, downtown Houston. The guy on the other side of the counter looked at me like, "Oh my God." Then he said, "Are you sure?" Then he disappeared for what felt like an hour and came back carrying these huge books.

And I thought, *Jackpot.*

In one stroke I had gone from the hit-or-miss of cold-calling to discovering a gold mine of people who were way more likely than not to subscribe to the paper.

At first I had to sit there and write down every name and address. But then I realized I could bring in my trusty Apple II (it was much lighter than the IBM PC), plug it in, and type in all the info.

And then it hit me that there were sixteen counties surrounding

Houston, they all had courthouses, and every courthouse had records of marriage applications. Jackpot times sixteen. I had wheels, I had a computer, and I had friends. So I hired my high school buddies to travel to all those courthouses and get all that info (some of them had their own Apple IIs that they could take along to get everything down, or sometimes they borrowed mine), and then I conducted a massive direct-mail campaign, sending subscription offers to every young married couple on that huge list.

Part of the building boom in Houston was that all these very large apartment and condominium complexes were going up. I would go to these places and say, "I'm from the *Houston Post*, and we've got this great offer where all your new residents can get the paper free for two weeks. Just fill out this little form."

Between all the young marrieds and the new apartment dwellers, I made a little over $18,000 that summer.

A story.

In my junior year at Memorial High I took a class called Government and Economics. The teacher was Mrs. Miller, and like Mr. Haynes, she hated me. Why? I'm sorry to say I gave her a pretty good reason. From my first days in her class, my routine was the same: I would come in, go to the back of the room, sit down, and read computer magazines. I wasn't doing it just to be a smart-ass; I was mainly doing it because I was bored—Mrs. Miller was talking about basic economics and government, which I pretty much already understood. But she didn't know that; she just saw me apparently goofing off, and she got mad. Mad enough to call my father.

"Hey, your son isn't paying attention in class," she said. "Can you tell him to straighten up?"

"Have you given him any tests yet?" my dad asked.

Mrs. Miller said she hadn't.

"Why don't you give him a test, and if he doesn't do well, call me back," my dad said.

ever wants to see. My dad shook his head. "Michael," he said. "Michael. You've got to get your priorities straight. You've got to get your head screwed on straight. This computer thing—" He hesitated. "It could be a nice hobby for you. But your life, Michael. Your life."

I was staring at the floor, ashamed and proud at the same time; obedient and rebellious. I had no idea what to say to them.

"What do you want to do with your *life*, Michael?" my father asked.

"I want to compete with IBM!" I said. I was only half kidding. But my dad wasn't amused.

"You are here for one thing and one thing only," he said. "And that is to get the education you need to put you on the right path in life."

I muttered something about not being so sure the path he was talking about was the right path for me.

Then I looked at my mother.

Her tears were flowing now, and she had both hands on the neckline of her dress. "Michael—" she began—and then she said my name again. "Michael."

The gesture she was making was more than a gesture. She actually looked as though she was about to rend her garment, an ancient Jewish expression of bereavement. Right there in a room at the Hyatt Regency Austin, she was laying five-thousand-plus years of Jewish guilt on my head. Telling me that if I kept going the way I was going, I would be dead to her. Wow.

Naturally, I caved.

I was crying; my mother and father were crying. When I was finally able to summon a semblance of composure, I blew my nose and looked at them. "Okay," I said.

They were staring at me. It's a pretty powerful thing when both your parents are staring at you like that.

"Okay," I repeated. "No more computers. Only school. Only school. I promise."

I really did mean it. But all I was feeling was pain.

———

For the next ten days I went cold turkey. I literally didn't touch a computer. No memory upgrades, no hard drive installations, no fly-and-buys. No *Byte* or *PC Magazine*. I went to my classes and tried my hardest to pay attention. I took notes.

For my tech jones, I thought it might help to turn my attention to another enthusiasm of mine, high-end audio. I loved listening to rock 'n' roll—Rolling Stones, the Doors, Jimi Hendrix, Queen, Roxy Music—and I liked it loud. In those just-on-the-cusp-of-CD days, audiophiles still went gaga for Thorens turntables, Harman Kardon receivers, big Klipsch speakers. In my spare time, I frequented the high-end audiophile stores in Austin, hoping the look and smell of those beautiful components would ease my craving for memory cards and motherboards and BIOS chips—not to mention the thrill I got from just being in the computer business.

It didn't help.

In fact, what those ten days of intense longing really did for me was focus my mind, intensely. I realized that the prospect of practicing medicine, in any specialty, held absolutely no appeal for me. And that the prospect of building my working life on computers was more than appealing—it was absolutely thrilling.

So I arrived at a very eighteen-year-old type of stratagem: I would go back to my computer businesses, and I wouldn't tell my parents. Brilliant, right? Besides, it was the eve of Christmas break: I could restart without having to worry about going to classes.

But it had become clear to me that a little dorm room on the twenty-seventh floor of a high-rise was grossly inadequate for storing inventory. If I was going to go back into this thing full bore, I was going to need a lot more space than I had up at the top of Dobie. Thus, with plenty of working capital still in the bank, I decided to get another place of my own.

At the beginning of January I moved into a condo complex a couple

of blocks north of campus, at 3200 Duval Street. It was the nicest building in the area—it had a gated underground garage for my Beemer—
and I got one of the nicest units in it, a two-bedroom apartment on the
third floor. I intentionally chose the top story, because the apartments
up there had double-height ceilings, perfect for stacking inventory. And
very soon there was a lot of new inventory.

By the time second semester began, I was back in business big-time:
upgrading, flying-and-buying, reselling. I decided if I was really going
to be a business, I needed to act and look like a business, so I looked up
how to set up a proper d/b/a structure, then filed the paperwork to become a sole proprietor doing business as PC's Limited. Not exactly a
genius name, but since my upgrades basically seemed to sell themselves, sexy marketing was the least of my worries.

My parents were something else again.

By the end of February 1984 I was spending even less time on my
schoolwork than I had during first semester. The time was clearly approaching when I'd need to fess up to my mom and dad. But right
around then I made a very useful discovery about a special provision in
the University of Texas rule book: namely, that it was possible to take a
semester off and then reregister at a later date with no academic pen-
alty. That was definitely something I could tell my parents, just as soon
as I got around to broaching the subject.

Meanwhile, I kept shuttling around Austin with my little crew of help-
ers, doing installations. On weekends I continued to fly around Texas
and Arizona, buying PCs and selling them back. The money kept coming in, and my overhead was low. My condo unit was right next door to
the landlady's—Liba Taub was her name. If she ever caught a glimpse
of all the computer boxes stacked to the 18-foot ceiling of my double-
height apartment, she didn't seem concerned. I was a nice young man;
I paid my rent on time. I didn't have wild parties.

During spring break that year I went with my mom and dad and Adam to England to visit Steven. My older brother, the smartest of the three of us, had graduated from college in three and a half years and gotten into Baylor Medical School, so he had six months off, which he'd decided to spend being a bartender in London.

It was my first trip abroad, and we made all the touristy stops: the Tower of London, Windsor Castle, Parliament. But I also made some side trips of my own, to look into what *really* fascinated me about England. For one thing, this was around the time that audio CDs were being introduced to the general public, and for whatever reason, the new technology had taken off faster in the UK than in the US. You could go into the HMV music store and buy lots and lots of albums on compact disk. I couldn't get over how clear and beautiful the audio quality was—and I couldn't wait to hear it through the big Klipsch speakers I'd bought for my new apartment.

But the other thing that impressed me was the profusion of computer stores—and, just like in the US, the profound ignorance of the people who worked in them. In England, as in the States, these stores were selling PCs consisting of 600 or 700 dollars' worth of components for the equivalent of $3,000 or more, and the salespeople knew little to nothing about how these computers worked. Nor did the stores offer much in the way of service and support. Neither the customers nor the retailers seemed to care. Everyone wanted computers, and the pounds and shillings were flying.

It was on this trip that my mom suddenly started feeling exhausted all the time. When we got back home, she went to her doctor and soon got the diagnosis we all feared: she had non-Hodgkin's lymphoma. But the cancer specialists at MD Anderson in Houston were hopeful, and so were we. We all knew what a fighter Mom was.

After we returned to Texas I broke the news to my parents. With all the assurance I could muster, I told them the truth: not only was I running a business that was consistently grossing over $50,000 a month, but I also believed I could build it substantially. And there was more good news, I told them: I could leave UT with no academic penalty and reenroll at a future date if wanted. I gave them my solemn promise that if my commercial venture didn't work out, I would go back to school.

I won't pretend that they were thrilled. There was a lot of frowning and head shaking. But eventually they agreed, grudgingly. It would take a few years for my relationship with Mom and Dad to heal. Still, they were logical people who understood a bottom line: they saw the logic of my choice even if they wished it otherwise. And the sad truth is that my mom was probably too tired to argue with me.

A couple weeks later I got a phone call from Kelley Guest. Kelley, a partner at a law firm in town, had bought a few hard-disk upgrade kits from me, both for himself and several other people in his office. "I've been thinking that you should incorporate," he said.

"How come?" I asked.

Kelley told me that if my business kept going the way it was going, I might soon be hiring people to help me on a full-time basis. Offering fringe benefits like medical coverage, he said, would be the surest way to attract quality people, and owning a corporation would allow me to set up medical and other kinds of employee benefits. He also said there were certain tax advantages available to an expanding corporation that wouldn't be applicable to a sole proprietor. He could do the paperwork pretty easily, he told me.

"Sounds okay," I said. "What's it going to cost me?"

"Well, I need another one of those upgrade kits," Kelley said, "so why don't we make a trade. I'll do your incorporation and you install the hard drive kit, and we'll call it a deal."

That sounded good to me. So I installed the kit, and Kelley drew up the papers. But then he called me back and said, "Michael, there was a small hitch. We couldn't incorporate under the name 'PC's Limited' because it's too generic. So I called the company Dell Computer Corpo-ration, and you can be doing business as PC's Limited."

"Fine," I said. "No problem."

"One more thing," Kelley said. "It turns out you've got to pay a thou-sand dollars if you want to incorporate in Texas."

You may think that with $60,000 or $70,000 in gross revenues every month, I'd consider a mere thousand a pittance. This was not the case. Not only did I have to pay rent on my condo, but as always, almost ev-erything I was taking in was going right back out again, primarily to buy new inventory. I was living on a pretty thin margin.

"I've got to go sell some more stuff," I told him. "I'll be back to you in a few days."

I sold the stuff. And on May 3, 1984, my little one-man operation formally became Dell Computer Corporation, d/b/a PC's Limited. It was just two weeks until final exams. I took them and passed by the skin of my teeth, then I left school forever.

A real business, I felt, should have a real office. Soon after I incorpo-rated, I signed a lease on a 1,000-square-foot space in an office com-plex a few miles north of downtown Austin, Unit F11 at 7801 North Lamar. And soon after that, I made my first hire.

Terry Hostetler was the manager of a local store called The Soft-ware Place. We met when I sold the store a demonstrator computer, and we clicked right away. We were both super excited about the PC revolution, and our interests kind of dovetailed: Terry knew an awful lot about software; I was more of a hardware guy. He was smart, he was mature—he was twenty-three to my nineteen, and he was married, which seemed very grown-up to me—and we liked talking about tech-nology. A lot. We even had similar senses of humor. I felt I'd found a friend.

One day we went out to lunch together, and afterward we drove around Austin in my BMW talking about our hopes and dreams. One of my ideas, I told Terry, was to buy a ComputerLand or Businessland franchise and leverage it into something bigger. In my explorations around town, I'd spent some time at a store called CompuAdd, which sold computer components rather than computers, and met the owner, a guy named Bill Hayden. Hayden told me that thanks to Austin's tech boom he was really making big bucks. I guess he thought he was just impressing some punk kid, but when I sized him up I thought I could do everything he was doing and a lot more.

Was I a little full of myself at nineteen? Sure, I was. I think you have to be to do anything important. You'll have realized by now that I'm a pretty competitive person, and I thought I had all kinds of ideas that Bill Hayden could never even begin to imagine.

One of my ideas was just an expansion of what I was already doing: placing ads and taking orders over the phone for memory kits and hard drive kits and upgraded PCs. I was constantly on the lookout for the lowest prices for computer components, and I felt I could save customers the trouble of comparison shopping, pass along the savings to them, and still make a profit. And my upgraded machines, which contained those components, were both better and less expensive than the IBM or Compaq PCs that consumers could find in retail stores. Not to mention the fact that unlike retail stores, I was prepared to offer reliable (and free) tech support.

Up to now I'd just been placing ads in Austin, but with a couple of people answering phones for me, I figured, I could advertise nationally—say, in *PC Week* and *Computer Shopper*, both of which had short-enough lead times that I could maintain control over pricing. Customers could call in from wherever and tell us what kind of memory or hard drive kit they wanted, or, if they were ordering an upgraded computer, tell us how much memory they wanted in their machine, what size hard drive, how fast a processor. Once they gave us a credit card number, we could send out the kits, or put together a customized computer for them in an hour or so and ship it out the same day. It sounds simple, yet nobody else was doing it.

Terry listened carefully to everything I was saying. He told me he too had dreamed of starting his own tech business in Austin, and that what I was talking about sounded cool.

"Why don't you come work with me?" I said.

He didn't hesitate. "Okay," he said.

It wasn't just me and Terry for very long. We started hiring technicians and salespeople right away, first a couple, then a couple more. Our little 1,000-square-foot office was divided into four sections: up front was a tiny showroom where local buyers could purchase kits or upgraded computers; just behind that were Terry's office and mine. Next was a space with four long tables: at two sat our technicians with their chips and cards and motherboards and drives and soldering irons; our salespeople sat at the other two, taking the calls that came in and writing up the orders on three-part forms. In the very back was a storeroom for computers and parts.

There were a lot of orders. The out-of-state ones came in on a phone number I was proud to have thought up: 1-800-426-5150 / 1-800-IBM-5150. (The 5150 was IBM's plain-vanilla PC, though we were also upgrading Compaq machines.) When we had a few kits and computers ready, we'd box them up and take them over to UPS, rushing to get there by five o'clock, when they closed.

As the business kept growing we kept hiring, about one new sales rep or technician every week. It soon got pretty chaotic in that little space, so when F1, a much larger office right next door, became vacant, we grabbed it. The new place had a bunch of cubicles for our salespeople and technicians and bigger offices for Terry and me, and right away everything felt more organized.

Well, sort of. Our order-entry system consisted of three clotheslines hung between the cubicles, with the yellow sheets from the three-part forms pinned to them. The top line was for orders that needed to be filled, the middle one was for orders waiting for parts to be delivered, and the bottom clothesline was for orders that, for one reason or another—sometimes parts were back-ordered—we had no idea how to fill. Our bookkeeping system consisted of piles of three-part form sheets and credit card receipts.

Terry and I each wore several hats. He was our resident software expert, also the office manager and bookkeeper. I sussed out the highest-quality and lowest-cost suppliers, helped answer tech support calls, and now and then pitched in with the technicians on upgrades. Throughout that spring and summer, as the business kept growing, we kept hiring, and the office was busy and noisy from morning to night. We were a ragtag bunch of computer buccaneers, and the sheer level of activity could get daunting sometimes. We kept a couple of foam bats in a box outside Terry's office door, and when things got too crazy, he and I used to slug each other with them to let off some steam.

It was fun, it was stressful, it was all-consuming, and I was proud of my little band of troops. But I was their boss, I was nineteen years old, and my experience of the business was different from theirs. And this was something that at that age, as I can see now, I wasn't fully equipped to understand, emotionally speaking. One Thursday that fall, Terry told me he was going out for lunch. "Okay," I said. "See you later."

Lunchtime passed, and Terry didn't come back. That seemed strange. Finally I called him at home. "I'm not feeling so good," he told me. "I'm going to take the rest of the day off."

"Okay," I said. "See you in the morning."

But he didn't show up the next morning, or the next afternoon, and on Saturday I went to see him. He seemed really unhappy. For a long time he wouldn't say anything. Then he looked at me. "I just can't take it, Michael," he said. "It's too much pressure; I just can't do it anymore."

"What do you mean?" I said. "You can't leave me. I don't know any-thing about the accounting and the software."

I realize now it wasn't the most sensitive response in the world.

Terry shook his head. "I just can't do it," he repeated. "It's just too much pressure for me."

I tried to get him to change his mind, but he wouldn't budge. I went back to the office and looked through the pile of papers on his desk, trying to make sense of them. Bookkeeping was a foreign language to me. For the first time in my life I didn't have an idea in the world what to do. I was alone, and I was afraid.

MR. DENALI

Super Bowl weekend 2013 was super memorable for me, and I never watched the game.

On Wednesday, January 30, at our foundation offices in Austin, Susan and I announced that the Michael and Susan Dell Foundation (MSDF) was going to give $50 million to the university's new medical school. It was a joyous occasion: our twins Zachary and Juliette were present, as were the chancellor of the University of Texas system and the president of UT. But I had to skip the reception afterward—the moment the ceremony was over, I bolted for my car and headed for the airport, where I met our CFO Brian Gladden, controller Tom Sweet, general counsel Larry Tu, and another one of our lawyers, Janet Wright, and flew to New York. Over the next four and a half days I spent almost every waking hour in marathon talks with the special committee over the final terms of the go-private, in what I came to think of as the Super Bowl of negotiations.

This thing had been dragging on for months, and Egon Durban and I were both pushing to get it done at last. The rumors about Dell had become relentless, and customers were seriously worried. United Technologies, for one, was about to award us a big contract, but with the status of the company completely unknown, they were starting to get cold feet. Meanwhile, all we could say was, "We don't comment on rumors and speculation." I kept trying to get Alex Mandl to move the committee along by telling him how unhappy our big customers were, but Alex, cool and tough as ever, refused to be rushed. He and I each had a vision of how to do right by our shareholders, but our visions weren't lining up.

The talks began bright and early Thursday morning in Debevoise & Plimpton's Manhattan offices, and they were intense from the beginning. Though Silver Lake and I had clearly demonstrated that we had the financing in place to pay what we thought was an eminently fair price for the company—I'd agreed to accept $13.36 per share for my 279 million shares, and Silver Lake was offering stockholders $13.60— the members of the committee weren't impressed. They questioned every detail of our proposal, parsed every paragraph. If there was any chance of getting shareholders a better price, they were determined to get it. Not only did they want to go out and find other suitors—the term of art for this process is a *go-shop*—but they were prepared to make an extraordinary offer: Dell would consider paying all the costs that any qualified suitor would incur in doing due diligence on us, up to $25 million. This was a highly unusual idea, to say the least—heck, it was a welcome mat. Then again, we weren't talking about your usual buyout.

Each morning Egon and I would meet in the lobby of our hotel, the Four Seasons on Fifty-seventh Street, and walk over to Debevoise's offices at Fifty-sixth and Third to do battle. There was a laundry list of unresolved issues—and at the same time, Alex was also saying, "What are the final bank commitments, what is the expected capital structure, and what about Microsoft?"

The special committee wasn't the only party we were contending with. We were still hammering out the repayment terms for our bank loans and Microsoft's $2 billion loan. Microsoft's largesse also came with a condition: they were unhappy with how many people in China were downloading bootleg copies of Windows, so they wanted us to forcefully increase the attach rate of Windows to the PCs we sold there. We wanted that too—bootleg software tended to cause problems on our computers. But we also wanted to settle on an achievable goal.

All of this is to say that between our lawyers and finance people and the special committee's lawyers and finance people—Debevoise and J. P. Morgan, plus Evercore, the investment bank the committee had retained as a second financial adviser—a number of negotiations were going on simultaneously. Every time there was a tweak to the deal, we'd have to get the banks to approve it, then bank documents had to be signed so the committee could see and approve the signatures. Couriers were kept busy. The emails were flying thick and fast, often until three or four o'clock in the morning. For secrecy's sake, every key party referred to in every document had a code name: Dell Inc. was Osprey. Silver Lake was Salamander; Microsoft was Matterhorn. I was Mr. Denali. This practice was customary in confidential negotiations—the names usually start with the same letter as the name of the actual entity or person you're talking about—but I'd first learned of it over the summer when somebody on our team started talking about Denali. "What's Denali?" I asked. "Oh, that's you," the person said.

Through Thursday, Friday, and Saturday everybody on both sides of the deal sat in that conference room at Debevoise and talked and talked. Sometimes we would hit an impasse over one deal term or another, and Egon and I would go out and take a long walk in Central Park to clear our heads before returning to the bargaining table. By Saturday night, February 2, I really needed a break, so I took my daughter Alexa, who was living in New York at that point, to a Knicks game at Madison Square Garden.

I'd splurged on courtside seats, which were great, but try as I might, I couldn't stay focused on the game. My brain was in overdrive: I just couldn't stop thinking about those negotiations, all the while striving, against all odds, to keep a poker face. I remember having the absurd thought: "Well, if I'm here looking like I'm enjoying the game and I have no other cares on my mind, then maybe they'll think the rumors aren't true." Easier said than done! Whether I was sitting in my folding chair on the Garden floor or going to the snack stand at halftime, I felt like I was in a mosh pit of interested parties. Spike Lee was sitting nearby—as was the head of a big private equity firm. When this guy saw me, he raised his eyebrows and said, "Interesting news!" Of course I knew exactly what he was talking about. And of course there was nothing I could say back to him except, "Yeah, how about this game?"

I returned to the hotel afterward, but sleep wasn't easy to come by that night. I'd expected the negotiations to be wrapped up by Sunday at the latest, but everything was still up in the air. We were at a point where either this was going to get resolved in fairly short order or it was just not going to happen.

At 1:00 a.m. my phone beeped as an email arrived. It was Microsoft saying they'd agreed to our proposal and were going to go ahead with the loan. That was one piece of good news, but we still needed several more. At 2:00 a.m., another beep from my phone: Silver Lake had sent a draft letter outlining two choices for the board: $13.60 a share if we continued to pay dividends until the deal was closed, $13.75 a share if we stopped paying dividends. This, the letter said, was Silver Lake's best and final offer and not subject to further negotiation. The next morning—Super Bowl Sunday—Egon and I submitted the proposal to the special committee, and that afternoon they held a meeting to consider it. When they came back, they told us they weren't interested in any plan that discontinued the dividend, and that they weren't satisfied with $13.60 a share. Alex told Egon that he'd have to do better. Egon told Alex that Silver Lake was unwilling to increase its offer. We were officially deadlocked.

Except that we weren't. Both Egon and I felt that there was play in the situation, and that despite Silver Lake's "best and final" ultimatum, Egon and his team could find a way to add a few more pennies to their offer. In the meantime I had to get back to Austin—I had several key customer meetings scheduled for Monday the fourth—and Egon had important business of his own to get back to in California. We both felt we could handle further negotiations over the phone.

On the plane home I got an email from one of our top sales executives with more bad news: AXA, the French insurance company, had grave concerns about all the rumors and speculation, and had just spiked a $150 million deal with us because of the uncertainty. The executive added that other customers were going to suspend purchasing from us until something was announced one way or the other. Meanwhile, all he could tell them was, "We don't comment on rumors and speculation."

The pressure wasn't just from the outside. Since our fiscal year starts at the beginning of February, every year around that time we have a big sales kickoff meeting (we call it the FRS, or Field Readiness Seminar, a name we came up with back in the '80s and had held on to for some reason), where thousands of our salespeople from all over the world come together to get training on Dell's new products and solutions and services. I was going to have to fly out to Vegas on Tuesday the fifth and get onstage and address all these people, and every one of them would want to know what the heck was going on with the company. And the last thing on earth I wanted to tell them was, "No comment."

I told Alex all of this. I said that our customers were alienated, that we were losing big deals, and that I needed to be able to reassure our sales force. Could we please get this done by Tuesday morning at the latest? I asked.

And as always, Alex refused to be rushed. "The dividend is nonnegotiable," he told me. "And the price is too low."

So we got back to work. While America was watching the big game, Egon and I and our various representatives spent Super Bowl Sunday trying to figure out how we could possibly raise our offer. By late that night—missed the game: Ravens beat the 49ers, 34-31—we were still deliberating.

As buyers, naturally Silver Lake and I wanted to pay as little for the company as possible. But we also wanted the deal to go through. Silver Lake figured (they were setting the price, not me) that adding a nickel to our previous offer, at a cost to us of five cents times 1.79 billion shares—$90 million—would make a substantial difference in the board's eyes, and wouldn't make a big difference to us if, as we anticipated, our thesis was correct and taking the company private would lead over time to a great increase in its value. And if our thesis was incorrect and we lost—and we didn't think we would lose—we would be out a great deal more money than $90 million.

And so early Monday morning, Silver Lake and I agreed to raise our offer by a nickel a share, to $13.65, and we agreed the company would continue to pay its regular quarterly dividend. Egon told Alex that this was absolutely, positively as high as he could go, and at around 10:00 a.m. Larry Tu sent an email indicating that Alex and Jeff Rosen (a key lawyer from Debevoise) would talk it through, then call Egon.

The NFL Super Bowl was history, but in our Super Bowl the game was in overtime and it was fourth down and inches to go.

Throughout the day and into the night of Monday the fourth, the special committee conferred with the Boston Consulting Group, Debevoise, J. P. Morgan, and Evercore. At 10:00 p.m. Alex and the committee had a conference call with Dell's board of directors and Debevoise—I wasn't on the call—and Alex, on behalf of the special committee, recommended that the board accept our offer. The board agreed unanimously. At 10:45 we received word that the board had officially approved the deal. After the call was over, our lawyers and the special committee's lawyers worked through the night to finalize the transaction documentation, and on the morning of Tuesday, February 5, it became official: our plan was to go private, with Silver Lake as my partner in a $24.4 billion leveraged buyout, at $13.65 a share.

ness was very important to me and this was a critical time during the go-private, but nothing would ever be more important to me than the needs of my family. The industry-analyst conference couldn't be called off, but if I left Austin early Wednesday afternoon, I could fly up to New York and have the family medical meeting on Thursday morning before heading to Toronto.

It was in the car on the way to the airport that it suddenly struck me: I was going to be in Manhattan for eighteen hours. Maybe there'd be time for a face-to-face with Carl Icahn.

And so I did something uncharacteristic. Without consulting my lawyers at Wachtell Lipton or even talking to Egon, I decided to simply call Icahn myself. Confront the adversary head-on.

I dialed his cell number, and he picked right up. "Hey, Carl! This is Michael Dell. How are you doing?"

There was a slight pause as he processed this strange turn of events. Finally he spoke. "Fine, Michael—how about you?" He sounded surprised, to say the least, but he also sounded kind of excited that I was calling.

"Great!" I said. From the tone of my voice, I was anything but a guy in the midst of traveling the world to defend the company I'd started; from the tone of my voice, I might've been a guy relaxing on the beach in Hawaii. "Hey," I said. "I'm headed up to New York for a quick visit— I'm just going to be there till midday tomorrow. I had the idea that maybe we could get together and chat about this thing. I'd love to hear your thoughts on it."

"Well, that'd be just terrific, Michael," he said. "Just terrific. I'd love to do that." Unlike me, I don't think he was feigning anything. He sounded genuinely enthusiastic. I could practically hear the gears turning in his mind: *Maybe I've got Dell where I want him. Maybe he's going to offer me fifteen dollars a share for my shares.*

"I got a great idea!" he said. "Why don't you come over to my place tonight for dinner? You have plans?"

"Let me take a look," I said. I pretended to consult my calendar. I looked over at Susan, seated next to me and texting with one of our kids. "Nope, tonight's good," I said.

"Great!" he said. "Listen, there's just one thing—I've got to apologize in advance. My wife really loves to cook, and between you and me, she is just a terrible cook."

"No problem," I said, even though it sounded anything but enticing. "We'll talk and it'll all be good," I said.

"That's great, Michael. I'm looking forward to it."

"Me too. See you tonight, Carl."

I ended the call and smiled at Susan. "Who was that?" she asked.

"Carl Icahn," I said. "I'm having dinner with him tonight."

Her mouth fell open. "You're *what*?" she said.

It was a beautiful spring evening in Manhattan, so I decided to walk from the hotel over to Icahn's place in the West Fifties—not just because it was lovely out but because I didn't want my driver, or anybody, to know where I was going. As strange as it seems, there could have been considerable corporate or financial ramifications if I was spotted dining with the enemy. The whole thing was funny and serious at the same time: I couldn't help thinking of one of my favorite movie characters, Peter Sellers's Inspector Clouseau, as I popped on my sunglasses and strolled across town to Icahn's apartment tower.

I didn't know what to expect when I rang his doorbell, but when the door opened, I saw an old man with a sparse gray beard and stooped shoulders, wearing a sports coat and pressed trousers. He smiled as we shook hands, then, shuffling a little, led me across his apartment, pausing for a moment at the kitchen doorway to introduce me to his wife Gail, who was indeed cooking. Whatever it was smelled OK enough. She gave me a friendly hello, then Carl led me out to a terrace with a view westward to the Hudson River. We sat down and he offered me a glass of wine.

"I'm good," I said.

He shrugged and poured himself a glass of wine.

"Nice view," I said.

He smiled as he sipped his wine. "Best in the city," he said.

Small talk was fine for me. *We'll get down to the nitty-gritty soon enough,* I thought.

First, though, came his life story. We were now seated across from each other at his dining-room table, eating our salads; Mrs. Icahn was still busy in the kitchen. Carl seemed very proud about having grown up in Far Rockaway, a middle-class neighborhood in Queens, and gone to public schools. "I don't come from money," he told me, in his strong New York accent. His father, he said, had aspired to be an opera singer but wound up being a cantor at their temple—which was ironic, Carl said, because he was an atheist. Carl's father seemed to loom large in his life, and not in a good way. It was clear from what Carl said that his dad hadn't treated him well, that he never felt good enough for his father. When it came time for young Carl to go to college, he was accepted to Princeton—a big coup for a Jew in the mid-1950s, when there were still restrictions at some of the Ivy League schools. But his father said, "Why don't you go to City College? You'll be closer to home." The point mainly being that City College cost just a fraction of what it cost to go to Princeton.

But Carl was adamant about Princeton, he said, and his father finally agreed to pay half his tuition. At this point in what I suspected was a well-polished story, Carl grinned. "I paid the rest with my poker winnings," he said. "Showed those preppie rich kids a thing or two."

And, of course, showed his dad too.

I smiled like the world's best listener as he continued.

He majored in philosophy, of all things, and—shades of my parents' expectations for me—went to NYU Medical School for two years before dropping out and joining the army. He began working as a Wall Street stockbroker at twenty-five, he said. "And seven years later I bought a seat on the New York Stock Exchange." He smiled proudly. "Worked my ass off."

By this time, Mrs. Icahn had brought us what she'd been cooking—it resembled meat loaf—and joined us at the table. She didn't say much, just smiled as her husband recounted all his successes. Somehow, though, his monologue then turned to his son, who was working for him. And Carl's proud smile disappeared.

"These kids today have it too easy," he said. "Everything on a silver platter. My kid's portfolio is loaded with Netflix and Apple, and he's minting money! Does he deserve it? I don't know."

At this point, as a father myself, I felt compelled to say something. "Carl, he's your *son*," I told him. "If all goes according to plan, he's going to outlive you—don't you want him to do well?"

Icahn shrugged. "Eh," he said.

"Last time I checked, living in New York City is really expensive," I said. "Aren't you happy he can pay his own way?"

He made a dismissive gesture. "Riding on my coattails," he said.

Wow, I thought. *What a dad.* I cut my meat loaf and ate a bit. Carl hadn't been far off about his wife's cooking. And I hadn't been far off in my estimate of him as a human being. We ate in silence for a little while, then Gail took our plates into the kitchen. It was time to get to the point.

"So what's your plan?" I asked him.

He looked genuinely flustered for a moment. "What do you mean?" he said.

"What's your plan?" I repeated. "You've got an offer to take control of the company. What's your strategy? Who's going to run it? Who's going to be the management?"

That's when something strange happened: for just a brief flash of a second, Carl Icahn looked scared. If we were playing poker, this would've been his tell. "Oh, I've got people," he finally said. "I've got candidates. A lot of people are interested."

"Is that right?"

"Oh, yeah. Sure." He dabbed at his mouth with his napkin. "Listen. Michael," he said. "Maybe we can do a deal, you and me. Maybe at the right price I'll offer you a deal."

Mighty big of you, I thought. "And what might that right price be?" I asked him.

He seemed delighted. He seemed to think that we were actually bargaining, right there at his dinner table. "Oh, a little north of where you guys are now," he said.

"How far north?"

"How does fourteen a share sound?" he said. "You could make a lot of money on this, Michael."

"And your plan for the company would be—?"

"Oh, you know. Economies of scale. Offloading unproductive acquisitions. There's all kinds of things to be done."

It was time to lower the boom. I looked him in the eye. "You know what, Carl?" I said. "I don't think you have a plan. I think if you want to buy the company for fourteen dollars a share, you should go right ahead. I think you're going to totally screw Dell up, and meanwhile I'll just go to Hawaii and take six months off, lose twenty pounds, then come home and buy it back from you for eight dollars a share. That'll be an excellent deal—for me."

He looked gobsmacked. He wasn't a guy who'd naturally come across as being insecure or fearful, but right now he looked like a guy holding a seven-high poker hand: nothing. The fear had returned to his eyes. What was he afraid of? That I might really walk away, leaving him with this giant thing he'd paid $14 a share for, this giant thing he was totally clueless about, and the team around him would probably leave as well. That he'd be left holding a very big bag.

But just then his wife returned to the table carrying a plate containing something that looked like pie.

"Carl, Gail—I'm really sorry," I said. "I've got an early meeting tomorrow." I stood. This was the truth. It was also after 9:00 p.m., and as a rule I turn in early and get up early. Icahn was famed for rising at eleven a.m. and pouring himself the first martini of the day. Not exactly my style. "Thank you very much," I told them. "This was a great dinner, but I have to go."

His wife looked a little taken aback. Now Carl was putting his hand on my arm. "Why don't you stay a little longer, Michael?" he said. "We've got a lot to talk about."

I was friendly but firm. "Sorry, my wife's expecting me," I said. "Thanks again."

If you'd seen me walking back to my hotel that night, you'd have seen a man who'd had a load taken off his shoulders. I was breathing easier, standing taller. *Wow*, I thought. *This guy has no idea what Dell does. Doesn't know whether we make French fries or nuclear power plants. He knows nothing, he's got nothing, he's just a circus clown. He's done.*

But of course he wasn't done—not at all.

Two days after my dinner with Carl came welcome news: Dell's board of directors unanimously recommended that shareholders accept our offer, asking them to approve the deal in a special meeting to be held on July 18. All stockholders who held their shares as of June 3 (the so-called *record date*) would be entitled to vote. In an open letter to the shareholders, the special committee called our plan the best option, offering certainty and "a very material premium"—some 37 percent over Dell stock's average closing price in the months before the rumors broke.

There was even a really weird period that spring when the board told me not to talk to any executives in the company. This was unprecedented. I don't think it had anything to do with the current business of the company; I think the board members were concerned that other executives and I might drift into the subject of the go-private, and I might color their thinking.

This didn't last a long time, but it was long enough. I remember wondering, "Am I supposed to go to the office or not?"

Right around then I got a call from Brian Krzanich, the CEO of Intel. "Hey, Michael," he said, "I just want you to know I've read all these stories, and I'm thinking about you. You're a really important customer of ours, and if there's anything we can do to help, just let me know."

I thanked Brian sincerely. We didn't need any concrete help from Intel, but the emotional support meant a lot. And there were other calls and messages of encouragement—notes and emails from friends and acquaintances and colleagues. I appreciated every one. But I'll always remember that spring and summer as a time when just keeping an even keel required all my concentration.

The proxy statement the Dell board sent to the SEC in support of Silver Lake and me spoke of the considerable business and transaction risks that a buyout would shift from the company to us. It spelled out in detail—yet again—the deteriorating industry dynamics for our PC sales, and the resultant decline in our key financial metrics. The stockholders would do best by cashing out now, the board argued.

On June 18 Icahn fired back. In an open letter to our stockholders, he announced that he was buying half of Southeastern Asset Management's stake in Dell, 72 million shares. This would bring his stake in the company to over 150 million shares, second only to mine. Surprisingly, the purchase price was only $13.52 per share, below our deal price and far below the $23.72 per share that Southeastern had argued was Dell's true value. Responding to the board's proxy missive, Icahn said, "We are amazed by these statements by the Dell Board. In what other context would the person tasked with selling a product actually spend their efforts negatively positioning the very product they are trying to sell? Is that how the supposed 'go-shop' was conducted? Can you imagine a real estate broker running advertisements warning of termite danger in a house each time a prospective buyer seems interested?"

Then he went on TV for the umpteenth time to press his case further. "Don't you think that the stock will be worth more than fourteen dollars?" he asked Bloomberg News, rhetorically. "Especially since the fourteen billion dollars spent in non-PC acquisitions haven't really kicked in yet? The company has put out these dire scary statements about its future. In a totalitarian state, propaganda of this type works. However, luckily for the shareholders, in our country, there can be someone to counterbalance the propaganda."

On June 24 he announced he was teaming with his financial adviser, the investment bank Jefferies & Co., to raise $5.2 billion in loans to back his $14 per share offer. He said he was confident the financing would be in place in time for the July 18 stockholders' meeting.

Super Carl to the rescue!

Or not.

If you looked through all the smoke Icahn was blowing, you quickly realized that his so-called financing was just . . . more smoke. As a piece in the online technology journal *All Things Digital* said:

> Of the $5.2 billion, Icahn and his affiliates have put up $3.4 billion, with $1.6 billion more from investment bank Jefferies and Co. An additional $179 million comes from fourteen other parties, including pension funds and institutional investors with names like the Public Employees Retirement Association of New Mexico and the Manulife Floating Rate Income Fund.

It's a relatively short list, Reuters said, suggesting that Icahn had trouble attracting interest, but on the other hand, there are signs he didn't want much participation from third parties in the first place. Confusing? Yup.

Here's another thing: Icahn doesn't get the funding unless Dell shareholders elect the full slate of twelve director candidates he and his partner, Southeastern Asset Management, nominated on May 13. Without that the funding is "unlikely to take place."

The unavoidable conclusion, yet again, was that Icahn didn't really want to buy the company at all. He was just trying to force us to raise our offer—and make his shares worth that much more.

But while Carl was spinning every reporter in sight, two big things went our way. On June 26, Chancellor Leo Strine of the Delaware Chancery Court—Delaware was where we (like many other companies) were incorporated, and the state's chancery court would ultimately rule on the deal—dismissed a raft of suits that had been brought by Icahn and Southeastern. In essence these breach-of-fiduciary-duty suits charged that I had a controlling interest in Dell, that I was working both sides of the deal, and that I was exerting improper insider influence. (In several of his many interviews, Icahn had even accused me of secretly being in cahoots with the special committee!)

Yet Chancellor Strine held that my 16 percent ownership didn't put me "anywhere close to the level of stock ownership that's ever been considered a controlling stockholder." If anything, Chancellor Strine said, Icahn and Southeastern together might be a more controlling force than me, since I had pledged to vote my 250 million shares in favor of a higher bidder, should one come along, and Icahn/Southeastern were under no such obligation.

Chancellor Strine noted that contrary to the class-action suits' claims, the special committee had exhausted every possible option in seeking a richer offer than Silver Lake's and mine, and that I had satisfied every legal criterion for cooperating with the committee. The result, he said, would be a comparatively lenient judicial standard when the Management Buyout Group's offer (ours) went to trial.

I liked this guy!

Chancellor Strine's opinion was a big blow to Icahn. But then came another.

On June 21 I went with Brian Gladden, our CFO, to Gaithersburg, Maryland, to try and persuade the good people at Institutional Shareholder Services (ISS) that our deal was the best one possible for the owners of Dell stock. ISS, the premier proxy advisory firm, is paid by shareholders to assess the kinds of proposals Dell stockholders were now looking at. The firm's assessment was going to matter a lot, and I took it very seriously—particularly because back in April ISS had issued a report that took a skeptical view of our buyout offer. "The overarching question," it said, "does not appear to be: 'How do we get this deal done?' But, rather, something with a much further horizon: 'If this is the best M&A valuation available, do we really want to sell at all?'"

I kept thinking of the meeting as the Battle of Gaithersburg. For a few mornings I'd been getting up extra early to study every possible angle of our proposal and to put together the strongest case I could muster. I came up with a list of arguments:

1. This is the company I started twenty-nine years ago and have guided ever since. It's crucial now to keep it on the right path and I care what's going to happen long after I'm gone.

2. I've seen the pace of our industry accelerate, and keeping up with it is critical. It's essential to control Dell's transition from hardware to software, services, and solutions; to mobile and the cloud. Transforming as quickly as possible is urgent: Change or die.

3. The changes we're in the process of making will provide the stability our customers want and the flexibility the company needs. But the risks we're undertaking will make the road forward a bumpy one, with inevitable setbacks—probably too uncertain a scenario for our public stockholders' tastes.

4. Transformation is rate limited for a public company.

5. The five new areas we're moving into and the investments required to make them successful will lower earnings in the near term. Many stockholders won't like this.

6. From the start of this process last August, I've made it clear that I'm willing to join with whoever offers the best outcome for our shareholders. And I've recognized that whoever offers that outcome may or may not include me in their plans.

7. A no vote on our proposal would be a vote of no confidence for the board, our management, and the transformation strategy, and would cause extreme disruption to the company.

8. Icahn and Southeastern say the company is worth more than our offer, but they've proposed no realistic alternative—it's all smoke and mirrors. They have not offered our shareholders even $.01 per share more than our offer. They've overstated their available cash by $4 billion. They have no real way to guarantee a $12 dividend.

9. Their so-called new management team is also an illusion. Both Capellas and Hurd have said they're not interested. Todd Bradley said he was never contacted about the job. Mike Daniels has a noncompete agreement with IBM.

The meeting went well. And on July 8 ISS announced its decision: it was going to recommend that Dell shareholders vote in favor of the deal. (A couple of days later, Glass Lewis, another proxy advisory firm, also recommended For. In a way, Icahn gave us both recommendations by creating an alternative so bad that ours was the obvious choice.)

This was a major shot in the arm. At the same time, I still wondered—and worried—could we get the votes? My uncertainty centered on a rule the special committee had set down at the beginning. In addition to getting approval of a majority of the outstanding shares, including mine, we also needed the approval of a majority of the outstanding shares that were not owned by me or Dell affiliates. In this second vote, my shares wouldn't count but Icahn's and Southeastern Asset Management's would. And abstentions and shares that didn't show up at all would effectively be counted as "No" votes. If the share price rose on good news (like the ISS decision) prior to the July 18 meeting, large blocks of stock were bound to be sold—and as the rules stood, the new owners of the stock, because they hadn't held their shares as of the June 3 record date, wouldn't be allowed to vote. But the former owners of those shares, having sold their holdings, would have no interest in voting—and their failure to vote would be counted as votes against our offer.

This voting standard was known as "majority-of-the-minority-outstanding"—minority referring to unaffiliated shares, those not held by me or my family and other insiders, and outstanding meaning all shares, whether voted or not. It was an extraordinarily stringent rule, but it was of a piece with every move the special committee made. From the beginning they had bent over backward to avoid any hint of collusion with me.

Three days later, Icahn sent out another one of his open letters. It was a masterpiece of wheedling. "Dear Fellow Dell Stockholders," it began, chummily.

On rare occasions in investing, one comes across situations that are "no-brainers." In these situations the odds are greatly in your favor of making a profit while taking very little risk, and in some very rare situations, you can make a profit while taking no risk at all. Strangely, in my experience many investors miss the opportunity to take advantage of these situations.

He was like a snake charmer (or a snake-oil salesman) in a carnival sideshow: Free money! No risk! All his fellow Dell stockholders had to do, he continued, was vote No at the July 18 meeting, then, if the merger was approved anyway, claim appraisal rights. And what were appraisal rights? Under Delaware law, if a cash merger goes through, shareholders who voted against the deal or who didn't vote have sixty days to decide whether to accept the deal or go to court for an appraisal. If this happened with us, and the Delaware Chancery Court ruled in its discretion that Dell stock was worth a higher price, the purchasing entity—Silver Lake and I—would have to pay the stockholders that much more. But the court could also determine that the stock's value was lower, and in this case shareholders who claimed appraisal rights would get less. In addition, anyone claiming appraisal rights would have to wait for the process to play itself out, which could take years. Icahn was just flat-out lying to say there was no risk.

What he wasn't saying, moreover, was that he had no intention of claiming appraisal rights himself. While appraisals are being resolved, it's as if the owners of those big blocks of stock are loaning the company the value of their shares! This was just another misleading proposal on Icahn's part, the transparent reality of which was that he was—yet again!—only trying to pressure Silver Lake and me to raise our offer to prevent those big shareholders from voting No.

And if you were paying close attention (and believe me, I was), the reality of Icahn's July 11 letter was that he'd basically given up on trying to buy the company himself. If he could get his higher share price from us, he could cash out and declare victory.

———

But neither Silver Lake nor I was inclined to be pressured by Icahn. To strengthen our cause in the week leading up to the shareholder meeting, I did some more traveling, flying around the country to meet with some of our biggest shareholders, like Franklin Mutual and BlackRock and State Street and Pentwater, to tell them why I thought our proposal was fair. And my lobbying got results: as the big meeting approached, BlackRock, State Street, and the Vanguard Group all switched their No votes to Yes.

The morning of Thursday, July 18 was a typical midsummer one in central Texas, the temperature headed for the mid-90s. Not a great day to be outdoors, though the pack of TV reporters with their cameras clustered outside our Round Rock headquarters didn't have much choice in the matter. Inside, at the appointed hour of 8:00 a.m., Larry Tu went to the front of the big conference room, looked around at the couple of hundred people gathered there, and said, "Welcome to the special meeting of the stockholders. As general counsel, I declare the meeting adjourned."

Just like that. Everyone was looking around like, "What just happened?" What had happened was that we simply didn't have the votes we needed to have our offer accepted under the majority-of-the-minority-outstanding standard on which the special committee had insisted. An email from MacKenzie Partners, the proxy solicitation firm, said that the count now stood at 539 million shares for the transaction and 541 million against. By the voting standard in place, we needed half of Dell's 1,476,288,661 unaffiliated shares plus one to declare victory: in other words, a total of some 738 million Yesses—which was about 198 million more than we actually had. Some 27 percent of all shares—over 398 million—had not voted, which meant that they were counted as No votes, by the majority-of-the-minority-outstanding voting standard. As long as shares not voting were counted as Nos, the numbers were overwhelmingly stacked against us.

That was a rough day. Egon had flown to Austin for the meeting, and when it was over he and I went back to my house and watched a big-screen TV, unable to look away from this 27-minute car wreck of an interview with Carl Icahn that CNBC kept running. Icahn and *Fast Money Halftime Report* host Scott Wapner were seated onstage at an Institutional Investors conference, and Carl, with his white whiskers and red tie and Queens accent, was in full nutty-grandpa mode—by turns defiant, shy, jokey, menacing. He often covered the lower half of his face with his hand, like a poker player with the world's worst poker face. His smile was strangely kindly. And the interview was vintage Carl: a weird, rambling mash-up of megalomania, hostility, complaint, and just plain free-associating. At one point Wapner listed some of the many companies Icahn had recently taken major positions in— Dell, Chesapeake, Netflix, Navistar, Biogen, Transocean, Herbalife, etc.—and asked, "Are you having, like, a midlife crisis at seventy-seven?"

Icahn grinned like the proverbial kid with his hand in the cookie jar. "Well, lemme ask you—what else do I have to do?" he said. "My wife watches me like a hawk—you know, she doesn't let me go out. . . ."

This got a big laugh from the audience.

Getting to the point, Wapner asked: "Do you think that Michael Dell will raise his bid amid reports that he will not?"

"You know something? I don't know," Icahn said. "And I will tell you honestly—I know you're not gonna believe it, but I don't care a hell of a lot. I would like to own the company. Okay? I own a hundred-fifty million shares—I'm in it to make money, obviously. But I would like to own this company, 'cause the real money I've made—you know, I was a kid from Queens, tough neighborhood, we never had anything, and here I am, so I love the country, I mean, sounds corny, but I'm really motivated to make money. But the most money I've ever made is when we control these companies. When we get into 'em."

He sure seemed to want to get into Dell. He was talking about fighting a proxy battle, installing a whole new slate of directors. And of course, a new CEO. "And here's why I think I can win," he said. "Because I honestly would say, if you're an institution, why do you want this guy still running the company? He's brought the stock down from forty to this number. So he mismanaged it; this board went and froze him out—you know, there's an old saying: 'Fool me once, shame on you; fool me twice, shame on me.' So if they go for [Michael] Dell again, then shame on them."

Wow—was it something I said (or didn't say) about his wife's meat loaf?

All of Icahn's takeover blathering would've been funny because it was so absurd, but what wasn't funny at all was the effect the chaos he was sowing was having on our stock price: in early July shares slipped under $13 for the first time since April; then, in the aftermath of the adjourned meeting, they stayed in the twelves for a week, then eight, nine, ten days in a row. The market was giving its verdict on the chances our deal would happen, and the chances didn't look good.

On July 22 I met with the special committee at the Manhattan offices of my lawyers, Wachtell Lipton. Alex Mandl was there with the committee's lawyers and financial advisers; people from MacKenzie attended as well. I spoke—and I spoke passionately because I felt strongly. As it stood, I said, the rule that counted shares that didn't vote as votes against the deal made the voting standard blatantly unfair, allowing a minority of shares to override the majority, based on those voting. The appearance the special committee had been trying to avoid—that they and I were somehow in cahoots, conspiring against the stockholders—had long since been contradicted, both in the financial media and the outpouring of open letters to our shareholders. We, Silver Lake and I, had clearly butted heads with the committee on any number of occasions. The lines were clear. It was time to make the fight fair.

And we found ourselves butting heads yet again. Alex told me that the special committee might—might—consider changing the voting standard if, and only if, Silver Lake and I raised our offer to at least $14 a share.

Meeting adjourned.

The next morning, after a long talk with Egon, I phoned Alex and told him that Silver Lake and I would increase our offer to $13.75—if and only if the special committee would stop counting shares that didn't vote as No votes. This was our best and final offer, I said. After conferring with the rest of the committee and all their advisers, Alex told me they needed some time to think about it. Accordingly, the shareholder meeting scheduled for July 24 was postponed yet again, this time to August 2.

Another bells-and-whistles Icahn missive, this one from him and Southeastern and sent to the special committee on July 23:

Ladies and Gentlemen:

In our years in business we have witnessed many unconscionable boards. But, we think that the ongoing "Desperate Dell Debacle" stands out as one of the most startling examples. Amazingly, through it all, the Special Committee continues to remind us just how much <u>they believe</u> that they are <u>taking care of us, watching out for us and protecting us. We have a number of questions</u> for these self-congratulatory champions of Dell stockholders.

<u>*WHY FREEZE OUT DELL STOCKHOLDERS?*</u>

Why is the Special Committee so committed to <u>forcing loyal Dell stockholders</u> out of Dell so that our company can be sold to Michael Dell/Silver Lake at what we believe is a bargain price?

How long can boards push out and change meeting dates and hide behind the "business judgment rule"?

The answer, my friend, is "Blowin' in the Wind". . . .

<u>WILL THE SPECIAL COMMITTEE KEEP ITS PROMISE?</u>

*On July 16 the Special Committee told us that it has **"taken extraordinary measures to ensure Mr. Dell's neutrality and to leave the final decision with the disinterested stockholders."***

*If you believe the Special Committee did not take **"extraordinary measures to ensure Mr. Dell's neutrality and to leave the final decision with the disinterested stockholders"** when they postponed last Thursday's vote, then we urge you to vote AGAINST the Michael Dell/Silver Lake transaction. . . .*

And so on and so forth, ad nauseam.

And on the following day, Icahn took the fight to Twitter, with one of his first tweets: "All would be swell at Dell if Michael and the board bid farewell."

Bob Dylan, he wasn't.

But did it get attention? Icahn always did.

Sayings don't create success, but we do have a saying at Dell: Failure is not an option.

We know great strategy and execution are what creates success. We were at the end of the go-private process: it had taken too long; it was disruptive; it had created confusion and uncertainty. And my allies and I were all—I wouldn't say exhausted, but we were very ready for it to be over one way or another. If the shareholders wanted a deal, we would find a deal and make it happen; if they didn't want a deal, we'd just go back to what we were doing. If shareholders voted for the deal they would receive some of the rewards of our potential success without having to bear any of the risks of the transformation. Silver Lake and I were taking all the risk.

In hindsight it's easy to point out that it worked, but it could've failed.

The same day Icahn sent his missive I sent out an open letter to our stockholders, breaking my silence for the first time in a few months about the battle of the past year. This was me declaring, Here's the deal, take it or leave it.

Dear Fellow Shareholders:

You have undoubtedly read many stories about our efforts to take Dell private. I wanted you to hear directly from me.

I believe that taking Dell private is the right thing to do for the company. We need to transform, and we need to do it quickly. The transformation is not without risks and challenges, and I believe that we can do what we need to do better as a private company than a public company.

When I came to the Dell board last August to ask if the board would consider the possibility of a going private transaction, I understood that the independent directors would control the process, and I made clear that I was ready to partner with whoever would pay the highest price. I encouraged every interested party to pay the highest price they could.

After one of the most thorough processes in history, the highest price that any of the parties was willing to pay was $13.65 per share. Although no other party has offered to pay more than $13.65 per share, Silver Lake and I have now increased our offer to $13.75 per share, an increase to public shareholders of approximately $150 million, which is our best and final offer.

I believe this offer is in the best interests of the company and our shareholders. Certain other parties have been proposing al-

ternatives such as leveraged recapitalizations, sales of assets and other steps that I believe would be destructive to the company and that I do not and will not support.

The decision is now yours. I am at peace either way and I will honor your decision. Our agreement requires the vote of a majority of the unaffiliated shares—your shares—to approve the transaction. Unfortunately, our agreement also provides that shares that do not vote count as votes against the transaction. Currently, over 25% of the unaffiliated shares have not voted. This means that even if a majority of the unaffiliated shares that vote on the transaction want to accept our offer, the will of the majority may be defeated by the shares that do not vote. I think this is clearly unfair.

When we offered to increase our bid to $13.75 per share, we also asked the Special Committee of the Board to change this unfair vote standard and allow the will of the majority of the unaffiliated shares that vote on the transaction to control the outcome. Particularly given the efforts of others to promote alternative transactions, and the ability of those parties to vote their shares when my shares do not count, it makes no sense whatsoever to skew the playing field even further by counting shares not voting as if they supported the opposition group. If the Special Committee agrees to our increased bid of $13.75 per share, and agrees to create a fair and level playing field in which you can decide, I will look forward to your decision.

Sincerely,
Michael Dell

Two days later, July 26, I went to Alex Mandl's house in Easton, Maryland, to try to convince him to accept our offer. I spent ninety tense minutes arguing to Alex that Icahn's bombastic broadsides were playing havoc with the stock price, that the continuing uncertainty about what was going to happen was corrosive to the company. That the bending-over-backward-to-be-impartial voting standard that counted shares not voting as votes against was obscuring the real opinion of real voting stockholders. Alex frowned and nodded, nodded and frowned. He heard me, but he never spoke a word of agreement. His own belief, he finally said, was that if Silver Lake and I were to increase our offer to $14 a share, the tide would turn without any need to change the voting standard. I said I'd discuss it with Silver Lake, but I wasn't optimistic.

Meanwhile, our stock continued to languish, and somewhere offstage (but not for long!) Carl Icahn was rubbing his hands.

UP, UP AND AWAY

Lee Walker changed his mind. And to this day I don't fully under-
stand why.

What made him give up a summer in the beautiful south of France to stick around hot and humid Austin, Texas, and help get a little computer company off the ground? I've asked him about it more than once. In his shy and modest way, he'll mumble something about having once been in the same spot himself.

When Lee was a young entrepreneur in the early '70s, he made a heavily leveraged purchase of a Buffalo, New York, steel fabrication business. Soon after he came on board, the company sold a metal-recycling furnace, a big-ticket piece of equipment, to a Florida customer—only to have the customer refuse to pay after the Florida Department of Environmental Regulation (DER) banned the use of the machine. The lost payment put Lee's fledgling company, operating on the thinnest of margins, in danger of going under, and Lee himself on the edge of personal bankruptcy. Out of sheer desperation, he flew to Florida and made a personal appeal to the DER—which, to his amazement, gave the machine a variance. Lee got paid, his company survived, and his entrepreneurial career went on to flourish. So he knew a thing or two about narrow escapes, and over the years he'd learned a number of hard lessons about corporate finance: an area where, in the spring of 1986, I was still learning on the job.

In certain ways, PC's Limited was doing amazingly well, given our fiscal limitations. Because I'd started the company with only $1,000 of invested capital—as contrasted with the almost $100 million that Compaq, our rival down the road in Houston, had raised from investors by late 1983—I had to figure out how to stretch the limited capital we had to the max. I got pretty good at it.

Our initial sales were usually by credit card. This meant that we got paid exactly when we shipped out an order. That was a good thing, but at first we often had to pay for materials ahead of time—hard to do when you have limited cash on hand. As we grew, however, we were able to convince suppliers to sell to us on terms, meaning we would pay them thirty days after we received their product.

In addition, by selling directly to customers and not having to build finished goods inventory, we could keep our parts inventory very low: if you know exactly what the customer wants to buy, you only need the parts required for those orders. By contrast, companies that build finished-goods inventory in multiple configurations and stock it in multiple locations find their inventory mounting up—and aging— quickly. By having fresher inventory, we benefited from the latest costs—and as material costs were almost always coming down, this gave us another advantage.

Credit card sales, paying suppliers on terms, stripping parts inventory to the bone: all these things kept our cash conversion cycle—the time it takes for cash to be converted into inventory and accounts payable, through sales and accounts receivable, and then back into cash— far lower than most other companies'. This was very good.

On the other hand, our fastest growth was selling to companies, government agencies, and education and medical institutions—entities that were not going to pay us with credit cards. We needed to extend

Alexa and I, 2016.

Kira, Zachary, and Juliette, 2019.

Susan and I celebrating
our thirtieth wedding
anniversary, 2019.

Chiat/Day created some of our best ads in the early '90s.

We loved going head-to-head with Compaq.

Dude, you're getting a Dell!

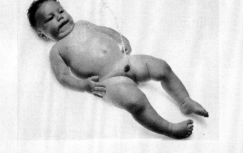

Piss on you!

In the past three years, Dell has introduced 47 new products, reduced prices by 58%, and *tripled* our market share. And we entered the Fortune 500 this year! IBM and Compaq, wake up and smell the coffee!

DELL

800-626-4310

Oddly enough, we never used this one.

The New York Times chose an odd picture to run with their story about the vote by our shareholders to go private.

Egon.

Joe Tucci and I on
the day of the merger
announcement,
October 12, 2015.

Chancellor Strine, the actions by Dell were within the Delaware law. We therefore congratulate Michael Dell and I intend to call him to wish him good luck (he may need it).

The charge that the board had acted dictatorially was another Icahn invention. By the time of the first adjournment, July 18, the special committee had decided our offer was best for the company—and, crucially, had not received a superior offer from Carl. The same was true on July 24, when the second shareholder meeting was adjourned due to lack of supporting votes. The committee had exerted all its strict controls and was operating entirely within the rules established at the beginning of this process. Its refusal to adjourn a third time proved its impartiality.

But I'll say this for Icahn: he really did call.

"Michael, it was a hard fight, but you won fair and square," he said, conveniently forgetting all the times he'd insulted my leadership—and by extension, me personally, accusing me, in the most public ways possible, of sheer incompetence, not to mention all kinds of corporate finagling and malfeasance.

"Thanks," I told him, though what I was really thinking was, *You came after this company, the thing that means more to me than anything in the world except my family, and you lost, pal. Thanks for nothing.*

"I really do wish you tons of luck in your new phase," he continued. "I've said from the beginning of this that I think you're doing some very exciting things at Dell."

I thanked him again, still wondering if he had any idea what our company really *did*. I listened for a few more minutes as he went on and on about God knows what—the prospects for IBM and Hewlett-Packard; how undervalued he thought Apple was (in a move that reeked of déjà vu, he'd just bought a $2 billion stake in the company and was already

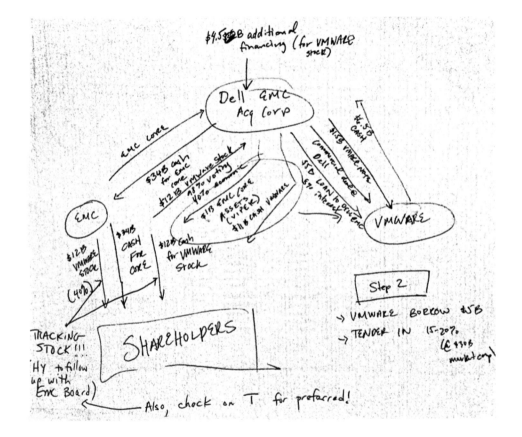

The historic paper on which Harry You and Egon drew the initial plan for the tracking stock.

PART TWO

Private Back
to Public

GROWTH, AND OTHER HAZARDS

Lee Walker's 1990 departure was the end of our first beginning.

After Lee left, the rocket that was Dell Computer Corporation kept rising, but our trajectory kept wobbling.

That year we ran a two-page ad in *PC Magazine*: the left page showed two of our servers, the 433TE and the 425TE, under the headline UNBELIEVABLE PRICES. The right page showed Compaq's System Pro 486-33 server, under the headline UNBELIEVABLE.

Our servers were priced at $11,799 and $9,599, respectively; Compaq's was listed at $24,698.

The ad copy hit Compaq with two hard punches: service and price. "Can you stomach spending an extra $10,000 for a PC network or UNIX workgroup server when the big extra is dubious service?" it began. It went on to describe our servers' many virtues: whisper-quiet 300-watt power supply; built-in password protection; software-controlled reset switch; efficient cooling system; our exclusive, built-in SmartVu diagnostic display, capable of identifying problems even if the monitor went down; more. Then the ad went straight at our nemesis, in bold type: "Servicing servers is beyond most Compaq dealers."

We, of course, weren't selling our servers through dealers but direct from the home office in Austin. And as always, direct was our brand, in sales and service. We had a special advanced-systems hotline, the ad continued, and: "On those rare occasions we can't fix it over the phone, Xerox technicians will come to your office with the solution or part in hand."

The ad wound up with a brilliant tagline, also in bold: "Above and beyond the call."

And Compaq kicked our ass.

Why did this early attempt at entering the server market fail? At the time I just couldn't figure it out—it was incredibly frustrating. We had all these great engineers; we were creating superb products. On paper our server initiative looked foolproof.

But over time, I realized what we'd done wrong. Our business was skyrocketing not just because of the excellence of our products, but also because of what had driven our success in the first place: our direct connection with our customers, from the sales experience through delivery, and afterward, technical support. And in this case we'd fallen down on the job. The 433TE and the 425TE were superb machines, so we thought our name alone, the reputation we'd built as a brand, would have customers clamoring for them. But the customers who were buying this class of product—medium-sized and big corporations; banks and government agencies—didn't trust us yet *when it came to this product*. Everyone knew we were very good at making PCs, but where servers were concerned, we had almost no track record. And that fact emphasized the second problem: the price difference between our servers and Compaq's seemed suspiciously big. We were charging too little! As one customer said, "Well, what if you left out something?" We hadn't left out a thing, but it didn't matter. Compaq had beaten us to market and established reliability—and as always, their high price signaled high quality.

We would have to come back to this fight later, and better armed.

In 1990 we also made a fundamental change to our business model: selling our PCs in discount retailers and superstores. There were arguments among our managers for and against the move: those opposed argued that retailers could never deliver the kind of service and support consumers had come to expect from Dell. What's more, the doubters said, dealer markups would either cut into our profit margins or force us to raise prices ourselves.

Those in favor cited the big rise in PC sales at discount retailers and superstores like PriceClub and Sam's Club, and the possibilities of reaching the many household and small-business consumers who shopped at these stores. People liked to buy computers they could look at and touch. Breaking into this market, some among us argued, could quickly build our brand name—and bring in $125 million in annual revenue. With an eye on those numbers, we signed agreements with CompUSA, Staples, and PriceClub to sell our PCs and peripherals.

And for the next two years, it looked as though the doubters had been wrong: our revenues just kept climbing. By fiscal year 1990, our revenues had risen to $389 million. Our ever more successful sales strategy of targeting big institutional customers—Fortune 2000 companies like Exxon and Dow Chemical and GE and Citibank, as well as state and federal governments, along with educational and health care institutions—had a lot to do with our rapid growth.

In 1991 we entered the Fortune 500, at number 490, with sales of $546 million: a very proud moment for me personally and for the whole team. We'd been in business for just seven years; I was twenty-six. Could I have imagined such a thing as a kid perusing those big, thick copies of *Fortune* that came to the house every month? Okay, I'll admit that I could have. I always did dream big. But I don't think even my ambitious younger self could've foreseen the threshold where we stood on January 31, 1992, when our sales for FY 1992 hit $890 million, and the fabled billion-dollar barrier seemed reachable, even breachable.

———————

My ambitious younger self certainly couldn't have foreseen my reaction when our first child, Kira, was born in January 1992. I was smitten with her, and with fatherhood, from the moment she arrived. I remember holding her in her room a day or so after she got home from the hospital and thinking, *Wow—this is a total game changer.*

But I don't think I understood the plight of people with kids until I had my own.

As all parents learn quickly, having a lot of new stuff to worry about is part of the deal. I certainly learned this lesson fast—when we brought Kira home from the hospital and she started turning blue.

Your first thought is, *Should we call 911?* But the baby was breathing fine; she was just blue. So we called my mom.

"Why don't you wrap her in a blanket?" Mom said.

We wrapped Kira in a blanket, and the blue went away—turned out she was just cold. Who knew babies turn blue when they're cold? Mom did. Now we did too.

That was easy. But not everything was.

The spring of 1993 saw our ninth anniversary as a company; Susan and I had been married for just two and a half of those nine years. Susan was a businesswoman, so she understood my laser focus on the company, my frequent distraction: if you want to win Olympic gold, you have to be fanatical. And if you want to have a successful relationship, you have to have love, trust, respect, and commitment. My wife and I both felt all those things, deeply—but that didn't make the inevitable imbalances between my work life and my home life any easier.

And life always has a way of taking unexpected turns.

One weekend when Kira was sixteen months old—it was mid-May of 1993—Susan and an old friend both celebrated belated bat mitzvahs. We had all of our family and many friends in town. Apparently someone found out about it and assumed we might not be home that evening.

We left the baby with her nanny, went to the celebration, and had a nice time.

After a while, Susan called home to see how things were going. But instead of the nanny, Officer So-and-So from the Austin Police Department answered the phone.

Quite understandably, Susan began to freak out.

With my compartmentalizing abilities in full deployment, I was able to calm her down enough after a few moments to take the phone and talk to the police officer. "Sir, there's been a break-in at your house," he said.

My heart dropped down an elevator shaft for a second. "Is anybody injured?" I asked.

"No sir, everybody's fine," the officer said. "Your daughter and the babysitter are fine."

Needless to say, we got home fast.

What happened: behind our backyard on Valburn Circle was a steep slope with a 20-foot retaining wall, to keep the house from sliding off the hill. It turned out that some guy had an accomplice with a dirt bike drive him up to the foot of the wall, then got off the bike, scaled the wall, and broke into the house through a window in the exercise room. We had an alarm system, but the only time we ever turned it on was when we all left, so it was off that night. We did have some cameras, but this guy apparently knew where the cameras were, knew the layout of the house, and knew exactly where he wanted to go to get whatever he wanted to get—mainly jewelry.

The babysitter heard a noise, and with Kira in her arms, went to our bedroom to see what was going on—and saw a guy dressed in black and wearing a mask. Somehow the guy didn't see her, and somehow she had the presence of mind to take Kira into our dressing-room closet, turn off the light, and hold her quietly. After the burglar got what he wanted and left, she called the police.

We'd thought the perils of my being a local celebrity in Austin were limited to the goofy drive-bys: the cars that tooled slowly past our house and the occasional well-wisher who felt it would be a good idea to come up the walk and ring the doorbell. But this took things to a whole new level. On the advice of Mort Meyerson,* I called Ross Perot, who was said to know a thing or two about security, and good old Ross snapped right into action. "Here's what we're gonna do," he said, in that crisp Texas accent—and he did it. He sent over the head of his security team, and we put a whole new system into place, with a guard in a gatehouse and 24-hour monitoring.

It was a scary incident, but it was also a very inexpensive wake-up call: what had happened could have been much, much worse. The episode was an end to some kind of innocence—I'd thought, like most people, that we could just live our lives and everything would be fine, but that turned out not to be the case. Fame is overrated for sure. But from that point on, things changed. Fortunately, in 1991 we'd bought a piece of land in the hills west of Austin and started designing a new home. It was time to put a little more space between us and the complicated world in which we were living.

We had expanded across Europe as far as it was possible to go—Russia wasn't really open at the time—and now we were turning our focus toward Asia, where two-thirds of the world's population lived. It was clear that our corporate logo, just a bunch of characters in an alphabet not used by much of the world, needed updating.

In early 1992 our new logo, designed by the New York design firm of Siegel + Gale, made its debut on our annual report for the fiscal year that ended on January 31. The new logo contained a seemingly minor

---

* Mort, who'd worked closely with Ross Perot in building EDS, had been an adviser to me and Dell Inc. until 1991, when he left to help Ross with his first presidential campaign.

change that would grow to have enormous importance to us: by tilting the E of DELL back 30 degrees, the designers had transformed a run-of-the-mill word on the page into a powerful and universally recognizable visual symbol, one that fit our growing identity as a world-class company.

As Siegel + Gale put it, "The new graphic identity . . . embodies the company's irrepressible spirit that stood the PC industry on its ear by selling directly to the customer." Or as I like to put it, "The *E* is pointing upward for continual growth and progress."

We sure had the growth part down.

On January 31, 1993, Dell breached the fabled billion-dollar barrier—and then some. When the results for the latest fiscal year were announced, we'd posted sales of not one billion but two billion dollars: $2.014 billion, to be exact.

It's said that companies hit the wall when they get to a billion dollars in revenues: the systems and tools required to run a billion-dollar company are very different from those needed to run a $100 million company. Well, we hadn't exactly hit the billion-dollar wall—we'd jumped right over it. And things were falling apart.

We were simply growing too fast. The different parts of the company each believed they were making their plan, but when you rolled up the results you had a big problem—in reality, there wasn't one part of the company that was fully capable of supporting the level at which we now found ourselves. We were outgrowing everything: our abilities, our systems, our people. And our capital structure. This new giga-sized Dell was consuming much more capital. One of the most important hires I made in that period was Tom Meredith, who joined us as CFO in November 1992 from Sun Microsystems, where he'd been the treasurer. I gave Tom a nickname soon after he arrived: The Alarmist. I was only half joking. Tom was deeply concerned about the rate at which we were burning through capital: our mantra, he said, was Growth, Growth, Growth when it ought to be Liquidity, Profitability, and Growth. In that order.

Change was going to be hard—we realized we would have to intentionally slow down our expansion and build more capability. One of the big challenges was hiring and nurturing the talent that could manage what was clearly going to be a multibillion-dollar business. We could see a path from $2 billion or $3 billion in sales to $10 billion. We actually had a plan to grow from $3 billion to $12 billion over the next couple of years. But how would we do it and who was going to take us there?

Our rapid expansion had meant lots of new hiring in every department: engineering, sales, manufacturing, technical support, finance, IT, marketing, human resources, everything. (We'd also increased the size of our board of directors from five to seven: in 1991, on Mort Meyerson's advice, we added Tom Luce, a prominent Texas lawyer who'd worked closely with Ross Perot; and in 1992 Claudine Malone, a Black woman who'd been a business professor at Harvard and Georgetown University, joined the board. I felt that diverse perspectives would help our growing company and wanted to make sure we had as many different outlooks as possible.)

Between 1988 and 1993 we went from 650 team members to almost 5,000, and we were adding dozens of new people by the week. But though we had talent on board—and in Jay Bell, Glenn Henry, David Lunsford, and others, we had really amazing talent—in those early days, with everything moving so fast, we hadn't yet been able to attract a solid core of people who could scale the business (to ten times its present size? fifty times?) with the stability and predictability it needed.

I was just beginning to realize that the people who got us from point A to point B might not be the same people who could get us from point B to point C.

We'd just barely survived our early financing crisis; we'd weathered the FCC certification crisis and the IBM patents crisis and the memory-chip inventory crisis. But now we were running into personnel crises, and they weren't pretty.

In the late '80s I'd hired a guy—call him Sam—to head up all our sales and marketing. Sam had a stellar résumé: he'd been in charge of IBM's sales and marketing and had built Big Blue's reseller program with great success. He then went to help Tandy Radio Shack rebrand its image and had done an amazing job there as well.

Sam came to Dell with a lot of impressive new ideas about our strategy of selling to big corporations. I put a bunch of younger executives under him, and he hired a bunch more. And Sam did some very good things for us—and then there were other things. One day I was walking down the hall, and behind a closed conference-room door (this was before we had open offices) I heard yelling and screaming going on. I thought: *Hmm, that's kind of odd—we don't usually yell and scream around here.*

So I walked into the conference room, and saw Sam, his face bright red, really tearing into a couple of the younger guys on his staff. The second he saw me, he kind of went from sixty down to zero in a second. "So what's going on in here?" I asked.

"Well, we're having a bit of a discussion, Michael," Sam said.

"Okay," I said. "Could you guys maybe keep it down a little bit?"

It turned out that Sam had a serious drinking problem. There was a hotel next to our offices, and the hotel had a bar, and every night he would go over there and get smashed, then get in his car and weave his way home. Pretty bad. For all I knew, he was getting loaded at lunch too.

Some of the other executives and I did an intervention with Sam and got him to go to a treatment program. But he didn't last long there, and he didn't stay with us long either.

Around the same time, we hired a senior VP of human resources—call him Ted. Ted came to us from Motorola, where he'd been very successful, and I thought he was a great guy. One day, after he'd been with us for a couple of years, another one of my vice presidents came into my office and said, "Michael, you're going to have to sit down for this one."

"Okay," I said, and sat down. "What's up?"

"We have a problem with Ted," he said.

"Is he okay? What's the problem?"

"Well," this VP said, "Ted has hired somebody on the second shift in IT."

"Okay, he's in charge of human resources—that's his job. What's the problem?"

"Well, we don't have a second shift in IT," the VP said.

"That sounds a little unusual," I said. "Have you asked him about it? What does he say?"

"It's actually a little more complicated than that," he said. "She's a stripper."

It turned out that Ted, who was married and had kids, had given a no-show job to his girlfriend the stripper. And the girlfriend decided she wanted more money, so she came to the company and said she'd need a good chunk of change to go away.

Needless to say, it was Ted who went away. What he'd done didn't just reflect very poor judgment on his part—of course stealing from the company meant he was immediately gone, no further discussion needed.

We were growing so fast—the number of people in the company was increasing almost as fast as our revenues—and growth covers up a lot of sins. It's sort of impossible to insulate yourself from the possibility of some inappropriate thing happening. But this was another one of those innocence-lost moments. I found it to be such reprehensible behavior— I didn't understand why someone would risk destroying his most important life relationships. I was probably naive, but I was also focused on growing the company. I would've never imagined that anything like this would occur.

I knew that it was my job to set the tone, that the tone at the top really mattered a lot. From that time forward, we instituted a policy that went something like this: If you're a VP or above, don't do anything that would reflect negatively on the company. If you're a VP or above and you're thinking about going to a place where women aren't wearing all their clothes, just don't do it.

Ted had failed the Dell IQ test: he was too stupid to work here.

With new products there are often many prototypes and iterations before a winner emerges. We test these products by previewing them with a small group of customers: starting small helps improve our batting average. Then once we actually introduce a product, we quickly learn from customer feedback at scale how well it's going to do. We take those lessons and keep improving. Each new product takes lessons from the prior generation in all areas: design and features, manufacturability, serviceability, etc. And the same process occurs in the company at large: in sales, services and support, supply chain, etc. The Japanese call it *kaizen*, or continuous improvement.

But for every company, Dell included, kaizen is an ideal rather than a reality. Success is not a straight line up. It's fail, learn, try again, then (you hope) succeed. How successful you are is really a function of how well you deal with failure—and how much you learn from it. Many people don't reach their greatest potential because they fear failure. In avoiding failure, they deprive themselves of a great teacher. Many others fall short because of lack of opportunity, capital, knowledge, or skills. Persistence is an all-important quality on the road to success. (And success presents its own challenges, avoiding complacency being the first and biggest. Which is why, along with kaizen, PBNS—pleased but never satisfied—has been part of our culture since the beginning.)

I've always kept mementos in my office, some of them personal— family things and such—and some that remind me of the company's high points and low points along the way. The low points matter a lot: though it's nice to remember successes, it's important to remember failures too. We've had some products that failed so badly we never even introduced them. One memento that I kept for a long time was a prototype for a mobile computer from the early 1990s.

It's hard to imagine today, but thirty years ago the truly portable computer was an elusive ideal. The first portables, back in the early '80s, were massive things known as luggables—they didn't have batteries; you had to plug them in. They were essentially portable desktops. The technology advanced, but for tech companies across the board, Dell very much included, the first several years of making notebook computers were not pretty. There's a video from 1990 in which Glenn Henry and I proudly tease our new 212N and 320N notebooks: there I am with my baby face and big glasses, solemnly ticking off the machines' great specifications: "World-class functionality; standard VGA display; full-function keyboard. . . ." And a weight of 6.34 pounds! At eight-and-a-half by eleven inches and two inches thick, those things were hefty little slabs of early-'90s technology—a comparison with our 2021 XPS 13, 7.8 by 11.6 inches and a mere .58 inches thick, weighing in at just 2.7 pounds, and with so much more computing power that it's hard to know where to begin to describe it, doesn't really seem fair.

As senior vice president of our product group, Glenn built our engineering staff from seven to several hundred people, oversaw a product portfolio that grew from three to over forty products, and, with a brilliant engineer named Terry Parks, established a big and bustling patent program. (Terry was brilliant, but *extremely* quiet: if he ever said a word, I never heard it.) Glenn was a great engineer himself, but I think it's fair to say that managing people wasn't his passion. He'd just sit in the conference room with a pile of spec sheets, drinking this wretched stuff called Tab and eating rice cakes, while his engineers streamed in to try to talk with him: every once in a while Glenn would look up from his paperwork and say, "No, no, you got this wrong," and send them off to fix it.

I was proud of all our products, but in the early '90s it was painfully clear that our notebooks were our technological Achilles heel. For a major campaign to revamp this key part of our business, I felt we needed new leadership as well as new ideas.

I didn't have to look very hard to see who was doing it better. After a rocky start with laptops, Apple had partnered with Sony to introduce its PowerBook in 1991, and they had a huge success with that machine from the jump, quickly turning it into a billion-dollar business and capturing 40 percent of all notebook sales. And the head of the team of engineers that had created the PowerBook was a stocky, funny, thirty-four-year-old extrovert named John Medica.

John was very, very good at what he did: one of his top skills besides electrical engineering was building and motivating corporate teams. He was a big personality who refused to take himself very seriously: his business card listed his title as Big Shot. Attracting him to Dell was a major coup. John accepted our generous offer with one condition, which I didn't know about till I walked into his office one day to find him sitting at his desk while this loud clanking—*CLANK, CLANK, CLANK*—was coming from underneath.

"What's going on here? Is everything okay?" I asked.

John smiled. "Oh yeah, I'm fine," he said—and then I saw the very large dog sitting by his feet, wagging its tail against the desk, *clank, clank, clank*. John's condition for joining us, I learned on the spot, was that he be allowed to bring his English sheepdog, Maggie Mae, to work with him every day.

A couple of months after John came to work, we added another key player from Apple: Eric Harslem, a vice president of Apple's Macintosh division, became the senior VP of our product group, succeeding Glenn, who took the new post of chief technology officer. Eric's assignment was to oversee development and marketing for our entire product line. He and John, and especially John, shook things up as soon as they arrived—and in 1993, they really needed shaking up.

In the first quarter of fiscal year 1994 (from February till early May 1993), our growing pains became painfully apparent: with our earnings down by 48 percent—our first quarterly loss since we'd gone public—and cash scarce, we'd had to withdraw a secondary stock offering due to Wall Street's lack of interest. Between January and June, our stock fell from a historic high of $47.75 in January to $15.87 in July. We warned investors that things might not turn around again for two more quarters.

We were going to have to make some big-time changes, and a lot of those changes were going to hurt.

Our notebook business was an especially sore point. Because our thriving PC business was taking up so much of our bandwidth, we'd simply failed to keep our eye on the ball where notebooks were concerned. The other major PC manufacturers were now getting 20 percent of their revenues from notebooks; for Compaq, the figure was 30 percent. For us it was 6 percent. Our challenges in notebooks also meant that we were late to market with a portable with the new Intel 486 processor.

John Medica's mandate was to make us a player in notebooks, and he hit the ground running. As soon as he arrived, he took a careful look at our current product lineup and the new models on our drawing boards and found both sorely lacking. The machines we'd been selling, the 320SLi and the 325SLi, were not only underpowered but had a design flaw—a capacitor that might crack under physical stress and overheat, possibly posing a fire hazard. And John concluded that the new computers, by the time we could get them to market, would be old news technologically. That October, he instituted a recall of seventeen thousand notebooks, put an embargo on selling any more 320SLi's and 325SLi's, and killed the new lineup completely. The financial cost to us, between repairing the old machines and spiking the new ones, was over $20 million. The effect on our morale was even more painful: for months to come, while John oversaw the development of a new line of notebook computers, we would simply be sitting on the sidelines of the fastest-growing segment of the PC market.

The costs of our notebook hiatus, along with the costs of improving our internal processes, were going to add up to a charge of between $75 million and $85 million. Maybe more.

In 1993 it seemed every piece of news I heard got worse and worse and worse. And I didn't tell anyone except Susan, but for a long time that year I was in a state of slowly rising panic.

Then a new year dawned—the year of Dell Inc.'s tenth anniversary—and with it came more help, and hope.

We'd hired the consulting firm Bain & Co. to help us navigate this crisis, and one of their partners, Kevin Rollins, especially impressed me. Kevin was a strategy guy more than a product guy—his experience was mainly with aerospace companies—and from the beginning he understood our business more deeply than anyone I'd ever worked with before. And there was one piece of our strategy that he immediately homed in on: our now three-year-old decision to sell our PCs through big-box chain stores like Sam's Club and Walmart. Kevin felt strongly right away that the dollars these retail sales added to our revenues weren't worth the trouble. He argued that with the resellers effectively acting as a barrier between us and the people who bought our computers in stores, a vital line of communication between Dell and these consumers was lost: we could learn nothing from those buyers about what they thought of our products' performance. *Direct* was our brand; this kind of indirectness threatened to undermine everything we'd built.

And so we stopped, just like that.

Some business journalists and financial analysts said—loudly—that the switchback made us look indecisive. But people are always going to say things, and there are worse things for a company than temporarily looking bad. We were in serious need of regrouping, and it was important to ignore the yapping dogs and stick to the plan.

Which was . . . ?

We were the fifth-largest computer company in the world. We'd made it past the $2 billion barrier, we were closing in on $3 billion, and we intended to go to $10 billion. I was all for meeting that ambitious goal, but part of me was also thinking, *Okay, now we're going to go to $10 billion? Seriously? This is getting to be a big damn company. There's a lot of stuff we don't know how to do here.*

I thought we needed some more help, so I contacted Heidrick & Struggles, the recruiting firm. "Go find me somebody who can partner with me in growing this business from $3 billion to $10 billion," I told them. "Somebody who has broad international experience and expertise in supply chain and technology."

Heidrick & Struggles asked: "Well, what's their role going to be?"

"We don't know yet," I said. Truthfully.

They started sending me résumés. I had a pretty quick gut reaction to most of them: "No, no, no." But some of them (far fewer) made me say, "Yes, yes, yes." Those were the candidates I met with. And the biggest Yes of the bunch was Mort Topfer, of Motorola.

Mort was fifty-seven years old; he'd been with Motorola for twenty-three years, eventually becoming president of their Land Mobile Products sector—aka walkie-talkies. This was just before the cell phone business blew up; Motorola's mobile products had multiple uses in industry, law enforcement, and the military, among other areas, and Land Mobile Products was the company's crown jewel, a $3 billion international division at a time when Motorola was one of the most esteemed companies in the world. Mort ran manufacturing and sales and marketing: he pretty much had the whole package.

And I liked him immediately. He was Brooklyn-born, and there was a lot of Brooklyn still in him, and I don't just mean his accent: he was warm and tough at the same time, and supersmart. He had broad experience in technology, and I also liked the fact that he wasn't itching to leave Motorola—he was happy there, and justifiably proud of his achievements. He and his wife had recently built a retirement house in Las Vegas and were planning to move there for good after Mort had worked a few more years.

He also checked another box for me. We needed to bring in someone at a very high level—someone who, in essence, could work side by side with me to lead the company to the next big milestone. If that person were forty-five or fifty years old, all the people below him would inevitably think, "I've lost my chance." But Mort (I thought but didn't say yet) could be a kind of wise hand or elder statesman: someone who wouldn't really intimidate anybody, someone who was just here to help.

Mort and I first met in January 1994, and we got together several times afterward, just to keep talking about how running a $10 billion global business would work. He wasn't auditioning; he was just advising me, and everything he said made a lot of sense.

Yet after we met a few times, I kind of saw something click in him— I could tell he was getting interested in the challenge of helping us rise to the next level. So I made him an offer, and came up with a title I thought everyone, especially Mort, could live with: vice chairman. Soon after he joined us we formed what we called the Office of the Chairman—the OOC—to emphasize the fact that he and I were working together.

Mort immediately went into operating mode, helping where we needed help. We needed help. One of our biggest needs was something he knew a lot about: we were going through a rapid expansion internationally, particularly in Asia. We were setting up a factory in Penang, Malaysia, and laying the groundwork for going into China, and getting going in Japan. And we were expanding production dramatically in Ireland (and in Texas). We weren't only building the business—we needed much stronger operational discipline, and Mort brought that, which helped quite a bit. He also confirmed my sense that Kevin Rollins, with his brilliant strategic understanding of our company, had become a de

Egon smiled. "And—this is the beautiful part—we really don't need that expensive mezzanine debt with Temasek."

Am I misremembering, or did Joe, Bill, Harry, and I all really break into spontaneous applause? What I know for sure is that now all of us were smiling.

We approached the rating agencies' advisory services to discuss our proposed financing and to seek tentative ratings for our financing and capital structure. Our final structure now included the rollover of some of EMC's existing investment-grade debt; but most important, by making Egon's bulletproof argument about VMware, we were able to achieve investment-grade tranche ratings for the majority of the new debt we had to raise.

This was a breakthrough. The investment-grade debt market is much deeper—being able to tap it enabled us to increase the amount and lower the cost of available new debt capital to a point where we no longer needed to raise any expensive preferred stock from Temasek to fund the transaction. Now we could see a path to victory . . .

. . . with one more major hurdle.

On Wednesday morning, September 2, Egon and I went to the Times Square legal offices of Skadden Arps for what was arguably the biggest meeting of my professional life. It was put up or shut up time, the day that the EMC board was going to take a beady-eyed look at me and my company and decide if we were worthy to buy their company— and, no pressure, whether I was worthy to lead the whole shebang.

It eased my nerves considerably that we had a friend with us: Jamie Dimon.

A big meeting room, filled with EMC board members and management and bankers and lawyers, a video camera and speakerphones to include all who couldn't be present: a couple dozen people waiting to hear what I had to say. I'd thought of the occasion as a job interview—I felt confident, but at the same time, well aware that there was a huge amount at stake.

The board had a lot of questions.

They wanted to understand our plans, and also see how things would change. They wanted to know how we would keep the VMware ecosystem independent. They wanted to know how we would continue the philanthropic and community involvement that EMC had at the core of its culture. I made my best pitch.

I explained how we could operate more effectively as a private company with a long-term focus. I mentioned the opinion piece I'd written for *The Wall Street Journal* a few months back, in which I explained how going private was paying off for us. In the piece I said that privatization had unleashed the passion of our team members, who now had the freedom to focus first on innovating for customers in ways that weren't always possible when striving to meet the quarterly demands of Wall Street.

Recalling the trials that Southeast Management had put us through, and mentioning the similar trials Elliott Management was still putting EMC through, I reminded the board that privatization also freed a company from the pressures of activist investors.

I explained our plans for team-member retention and growth. I said that we planned to retain the vast majority of the senior executives because our combination was mostly about growth and revenue synergies—and I reminded the board that HP would have eliminated many positions. The vast majority of the very talented people at EMC and VMware and Pivotal, I told the board, were complementary with our teams.

I affirmed my and our commitment to Boston and Massachusetts: I told them, as I'd told Jack, that I planned to get an apartment in Boston. I promised we would carry on the great work EMC had started in connecting with the communities that surrounded it—things like partnering with the state to bring STEM (science, technology, engineering, math) education and inspiration to K–12 schools; donating millions to local charities; and volunteering thousands of hours to help support environmental protection and disaster relief. I pledged that we would honor, preserve, and celebrate the company's strong culture. I said that I had profound respect for what Joe and his team had created, as well as how they created it, and that we only planned to extend it, not alter it.

An hour or so into the meeting, there was a momentary silence. Then one of the board members broke it with a question.

"This merger would add a lot to your job, and your job is already big," he said. "We're all kind of wondering how devoted to it you're going to be able to be."

"Look, this business has my name on it; it's been my life," I said. Then I smiled. "But also, those of you with kids will understand—my twins are grown up, they're both off to college now—I have a lot of free time on my hands."

This got a laugh. But once the room quieted down, another director gave me a serious look. "Do you have the money?" he asked. "We're talking about a lot of money."

Before I could say a word, Jamie spoke up.

"Yes," he said. "They have the money."

The laughter was even louder this time. Then another silence, as the stature and credibility of the man who'd spoken sank in. It was a moment I will never forget, and something for which I'll always be grateful to Jamie.

After the meeting I called each of the top EMC and VMware executives and asked for their commitment to stay with the new company. Every single one of them said yes.

We were closing in. And it was starting to get very real.

I went back to Austin and then on Saturday the fifth left for a weeklong business trip to visit some of our locations in Asia. First stop, Bangalore. My dad came along with me, as he would from time to time. It gave us a great opportunity to spend some time together; he could enjoy some sightseeing, and he loved tailing along and seeing me in action. When people asked him who he was, he would proudly say, "I'm the founder of the founder."

From Bangalore we proceeded to Shanghai, then Tokyo. Then Dad went back to Houston and I met Susan that weekend at a small resort in the wilderness and isolation of southern Utah where we love to go hiking.

Maybe it was also the jet lag, but with the announcement of the largest technology acquisition ever now about a month away and approaching fast, I woke up in the middle of the night with my heart racing and my mind swarming with a blizzard of thoughts about things I needed to do, and questions about how I was going to get it all done. The truth is that deep down, I wasn't sure how the whole thing would work. There were so many details to be ironed out, details that only a few people knew about, so I couldn't involve the broader team in addressing all of them. I am not prone to panic, but—I'd never experienced anything quite like it—this might have been my version of a panic attack. I wrote down a bunch of thoughts, stared at the stars for a while, and finally was able to go back to sleep.

On the morning of Monday, October 12, 2015, we made the big announcement: in a deal twice as large as the previously largest tech-only deal (HP's $33 billion acquisition of Compaq in 2002), Dell Inc. and EMC had become one company, with over 150,000 team members, to be called Dell Technologies and to be led by me. We had actually brought it off, actually purchased a $67 billion company with $4.5 billion in equity (plus all the equity in Dell Inc.). Our debt financing had succeeded beyond our dreams. It was as though we'd ridden a motorcycle over a tightrope across Niagara Falls.

The blowback began immediately.

Our competitors were saying, "Oh, it's going to take them years to sort it out; it's not going to work; they'll have all kinds of problems; you should buy from us instead."

Meg Whitman led the charge, as she had before with our go-private. In an email sent to "All Hewlett Packard Enterprise Employees," she called the merger "a good thing for Hewlett Packard Enterprise and an opportunity for us to seize the moment."

A good thing for HP but a bad thing for Dell, Meg claimed:

> To pay back the interest on the $50 billion of debt that the new combined company will have on their balance sheet, Dell will need to pay roughly $2.5 billion a year in interest alone. That's $2.5 billion that they will allocate away from R&D and other business critical activities, which will keep them from better serving their customers.

Meg seemed to know an awful lot about how we allocated capital! (In truth, our creative and efficient capital structure set the stage for strong cash flow and accelerated debt paydown.) But our supposedly excessive debt load was far from her only critique. There was also the problematic combining of our two companies:

> Integrating EMC and Dell, which combined have more than $75 billion in revenue and nearly 200,000 employees, is no small feat. This will be a massive undertaking and an enormous distraction for employees and their management team as two very different cultures come together, leadership teams shift and an entirely new strategy is developed.

Nor was that all. "Bringing two portfolios together," Meg claimed,

> will require a significant amount of product rationalization,
> which will be disruptive to their business and create confu-
> sion for their customers. . . . Customers simply will not know
> if the products they are buying today from either company will
> be supported in eighteen months.

Was the pot calling the kettle black? As one commentator wrote, "If anyone would know about that kind of mess, it would be HP." That huge acquisition of Compaq—admittedly well before Meg's tenure—had never amounted to much except the dismantling of a formerly import-ant company and a boost to our position in the PC market.

And then there was HP's purchase of the software company Autonomy—a company we'd briefly considered acquiring but passed on because at $11 billion it seemed outrageously overpriced. Appar-ently HP's board felt the same way because they fired Leo Apotheker for saying he planned to buy it. Then, one month after taking over from Apotheker, Meg Whitman went ahead and acquired Autonomy anyway, at the previously agreed price—and then the whole thing turned into an embarrassing fiasco for Hewlett-Packard (and an $8 billion write-off) when it was discovered that Autonomy had been cooking its books.

I do like and respect Meg, but what she was engaging in now was nothing but sowing FUD, in a somewhat desperate effort to make up for the other colossal blunder she'd committed, dropping HP's acquisition of EMC. Not vitriolic, Carl Icahn–level FUD, but FUD just the same. In her defense, this is something many CEOs do from time to time: I might have done it a time or two myself. She was just trying to spin the media and rally her troops. But the moment she split her company in two was the moment she admitted that in effect she had ceded victory in the IT infrastructure business to us.

———

We announced the merger that October, yet due to a long, drawn-out approval process—all the major governments where both companies did business had to declare that the combination violated no antitrust regulations—it wouldn't actually become effective until eleven months later, September 2016.

A story. By August 2016 every single country in the world where we needed to get approval for the merger—over twenty—had given their blessing. Except one: China. The People's Republic had not given its OK within the mandated 180-day approval period, and so had opened another 180-day period in which to do further analysis. Another six months of delay would be damaging to our business and our team, so I instructed Rich Rothberg, our general counsel at the time, to go to Beijing, report back to me every week, and do everything he could to make sure MOFCOM, the Chinese antitrust authority, had all the information it needed to come to a quick decision.

After one week, Rich called and told me that he wasn't hearing anything about when the authority would decide. The same thing after week two. When he called with the same news again in week three I told him that we needed to put a stake in the ground and tell MOFCOM that he wasn't going to leave China until they provided approval, no matter how long it took. Rich met my directive with about 20 seconds of silence, while he no doubt contemplated spending the next several months in Beijing and enjoying Thanksgiving, the Christmas holiday, and New Year's with our Dell China team members. He replied that he didn't think MOFCOM or the government of China would care about or be influenced by his whereabouts while they took their time deciding our fate. Undeterred by Rich's lack of faith in the power of one individual to make a difference, I responded that I also thought it would be meaningful to our management team, and a sign of how important this was to the company, for him to announce to our team his decision to stay in China until approval was received.

Another 20 seconds of silence—after which Rich said he felt confident that what he was doing in China (largely waiting in a conference room in our Dell offices) could be done just as effectively in Austin. This time I was silent, and after about 20 more seconds (during which time I'm sure Rich thought about the wisdom of his boss's "suggestion") he piped up that, in fact, he did think his remaining in Beijing made sense and would be a strong signal to the Chinese government that we would do whatever it took to get a timely decision. I'm not sure if that decision was a factor or not, but luckily for Rich (and for the company), MOFCOM gave its approval within the next ten days, and Rich was home in early September, in plenty of time for the holidays.

Throughout the approval process we knew our competitors were going to try to throw sand in the gears. We knew they would go to the Department of Justice's Antitrust Division and say, "You know, Dell is going to buy VMware, and they're going to take away VMware access for all its competitors, so you need to investigate that." So one of the first things I had to do was personally call the CEOs of all our competitors—the heads of Cisco, IBM, NetApp, Lenovo, and many others, and yes, Meg Whitman—and assure them that VMware was going to remain independent.

Then I really had my work cut out for me.

To put it in a more positive way, the lengthy approval process gave us more time to begin work on the very big and very important job of melding Dell and EMC. Because in truth, Meg's second point—that integrating two gigantic companies, each with its own distinctive corporate culture, is a bear—wasn't far off the mark. But she'd cast the challenge in the most negative light possible, whereas I saw it as a tremendous opportunity.

And before anything else, a branding opportunity. One of the big questions early on was, What would we call the new company?

It was not a question that could be answered easily or intuitively. So we applied a proven Dell process that resolves any decision, no matter how complex, in thirty to forty days. The process consists of two steps: Facts and Alternatives, and Choices and Commitments.

Companies often get hung up on big, complicated decisions, which either never get decided or take four or five or ten months to work out. Our way says, "Let's get the real facts here—not opinions, facts." At the same time, we ask, "What are all the legitimate alternatives? Not crazy things that you would never do, but the actual legitimate alternatives?" Then you spend not much time, a couple of weeks, looking carefully at each of these alternatives.

Then comes Choices and Commitments, which—no surprise—says, "Okay, we're going to make a choice and commit to it." The selection isn't based on personalities or emotions. It's a very fact- and data-oriented objective process. We have a truth-seeking culture, having learned long ago that facts and data are your friends.

With this branding, the first question was, What are the alternatives? Well, you could just call the company Dell. You could call it EMC. You could call it DellEMC. You could call it Dell-EMC-VMware. We had a few others: Dell Labs, or Dell Laboratories.

One of the alternatives was to create a completely new brand. But we concluded that that would cost hundreds of millions of dollars, and take a long time, whereas we already had one of the most recognized brandmarks in the world in Dell. EMC wasn't quite as well known across the industry, but to a particular kind of customer it was prominent and highly valued. All these companies with the big buildings with their logos on them—they knew what was in their data center. So for the infrastructure business, we created DellEMC as the brand, and then, as the parent company brand, Dell Technologies.

But even more important than naming the new company was forming a completely integrated and smoothly functioning team. Toward that end I spent the rest of 2015 and the first three quarters of 2016 going on a major charm offensive, doing everything I could to make as many levels as possible of EMC management not just comfortable about the combination, but excited about it.

One of the first challenges was to avoid—really, to stamp out—any characterization of the merger as an acquisition.

I always like to look at these things through the lenses of the customer and the team member, also known as the employee. If you're a customer, you don't want to hear about acquisitions. Carl Icahn makes acquisitions. These are the kind of takeovers in which entire boards and executive teams get stripped out in the interests of flipping a company for a quick profit. "A combination" sounds a lot better than "an acquisition." "A merger" kind of sounds like "a combination." You can say "merger."

Still, if you're a team member, maybe especially if you're a team member—there's something very odd about being in a merger. When you join a company, you've made an affirmative decision to join that company, and it has made an affirmative decision to have you join. In an acquisition or merger, that's not the case. Your company was bought or combined with another company and now you work for this new company. You didn't make a positive decision to work for this new organization, and they didn't make a positive decision to hire you, either. It's a totally different relationship, one that's tricky to make people feel good about.

What if the shoe had been on the other foot? I spent time thinking about that. We're sitting there in Round Rock, Texas, doing our thing, then some company buys our company. Well, first of all, the new headquarters wouldn't be in Round Rock, Texas, anymore; it'd be in some other place. And maybe I would be there, maybe I wouldn't be there, maybe there'd be a whole other set of people there. It'd be different, for sure.

And so I went out of my way during that year to give as many of EMC's people as possible the biggest hug imaginable. Of course, they had financial incentives to stay, but that isn't as powerful as the emotional connection, the feeling of, "Okay, I know the folks who are involved in leading this company, and I trust them, and I believe in what we're doing, and what we are doing is important."

I did all kinds of things. I took people to dinner. I invited people to my house. I wanted to build relationships and understand their perspectives and insights. From our previous alliance, I knew some of EMC's executives, like Bill Scannell (who'd started at the company back in 1986) and Howard Elias, and I had gotten to know many more during the past year. It was an awesome, very talented leadership team. I went on LinkedIn and connected with everybody who had a reasonably important title at EMC and VMware and Pivotal. Nobody expected that: "You have a LinkedIn request from Michael Dell." Not to puff up my personal importance, but people are excited to hear directly from the CEO, whoever he or she is. When someone would write me back, I'd say, "Welcome to the team! We're so excited, heard great things about you"—assuming I had. And "Can't wait to work with you!"

I also went around to as many of EMC's offices as I possibly could, always sending the word ahead of time: "I want to meet one-on-one with as many of the top people as I can." I wasn't disingenuous about it. I wouldn't tell somebody I'd heard they were great if I hadn't heard they were great, but my campaign was purposeful. I recognized that these people hadn't affirmatively decided to work for our company; maybe they didn't know anything about our company except what they'd heard. So it was almost as if I was rehiring every one of them. I was going more than halfway across the table to say, "Hey, I've heard terrific things about you, and I really want you on the team. I want to assure you that you've got an important role in the company—a big part of why we're combining is the work you're doing." And "This new product is really great; I want to learn more about this, and keep me posted on that, and feel free to contact me at any time and let me know how I can be helpful." I also wanted to hear their ideas about the best opportunities ahead of us. My note with everyone I met was, "We're in this together."

But my campaign was also targeted. We'd known since the beginning that the merger would create some redundancies: we didn't want everybody to stay. In some cases there were overlapping functions, and some hard decisions had to be made. This wasn't the key plot of the combination, but it needed to be done.

How do you decide who stays and who goes? We started with strategy, structure, people. What's the strategy? What's the best structure to execute it? And then, who best fits the structure to execute the strategy? As we looked at the people in both organizations, we found an incredibly deep bench of talent—for almost every position, we had three or four, in some cases five, qualified candidates. It's inevitable that when you put together two giant companies, there are going to be more great people than there are great jobs.

On the one hand, this gave us the opportunity to really increase the caliber of the talent across the organization. On the other, it made for some tough moments.

There was one top function—I won't say which—that was occupied in Dell and EMC, respectively, by two extremely skillful and engaging guys. Dell's guy had just been appointed; EMC's guy had been there a long time. Either one could've done an outstanding job going forward. But the hard truth was that the Dell guy, being newly appointed, was in a position to grow up in a role where all he knew was the combined organization, and thus could give the merged companies a perspective that wasn't steeped in one legacy company or another.

I told the EMC guy right off that there wasn't going to be a job for him. I thanked him for all the great work he'd done, and said I knew he was going to continue to help through the completion of the combination. I told him we'd have a generous severance package for him.

have helped me immensely along the way. I can't do much of anything by myself, but as a team we are unstoppable.

There are too many colleagues, board members, and advisers to name but some current and former ones have been absolutely essential—and sometimes pivotal—in the company's evolution and success. I would like to especially acknowledge Kaye Banda, Paul Bell, Marc Benioff, Jim Breyer, Jeremy Burton, Don Carty, Janet Clark, Don Collis, Laura Conigliaro, Jamie Dimon, Dave Dorman, Ken Duberstein, Egon Durban, Steve Felice, Glenn Fuhrman, Bill Gates, Brian Gladden, Bill Green, Tom Green, Kelley Guest, Marius Haas, Eric Harslem, Glenn Henry, Paul Hirschbiel, Bobby Inman, Joel Kocher, Sallie Krawcheck, Ellen Kullman, Mike Lambert, Susan Larson, Tom Luce, Kate Ludeman, Klaus Luft, Manny Maceda, Claudine Malone, Alex Mandl, Joe Marengi, Paul Maritz, Bill McDermott, Paul McKinnon, Tom Meredith, Mort Meyerson, Shantanu Narayan, Sam Nunn, Ro Parra, Simon Patterson, Ross Perot Jr., Karen Quintos, Rory Read, Kevin Rollins, Steve Rosenblum, Julie Sackett, Rick Salwen, John Swainson, Mary Alice Taylor, Mort Topfer, Larry Tu, Joe Tucci, Suresh Vaswani, Lynn Vojvodich, Lee Walker, Chuck Whitten, and Harry You.

I feel an especially poignant gratitude to those who have left us: the late Jay Bell, Andy Grove, Andrew Harris, Michael Jordan, George Kozmetsky, Jimmy Lee, John Medica, and Michael Miles.

And I want to thank all the present-day leaders of Dell Technologies, including Jeff Boudreau, Kevin Brown, Sam Burd, John Byrne, Michael Collins, Mike Cote, Steve Crowe, Rola Dagher, Mike DeMarzo, Allison Dew, Stephanie Durante, Howard Elias, Jenn Felch, Sam Grocott, John Haynes, Aongus Hegerty, Dennis Hoffman, David Kennedy, Adrian McDonald, Yvonne McGill, Maya McReynolds, Amit Midha, Steve Price, Brian Reaves, Rich Rothberg, Jennifer Saavedra, Bill Scannell, Doug Schmidt, Tom Sweet, Gerri Tunnell, and so many others.

Pat Gelsinger, who was so crucial to the rise of VMware and the early years of the merged Dell-EMC—and who has now returned, with poetic justice, to Intel—deserves a special mention.

I must single out Jeff Clarke. Having joined the company in 1987, Jeff is the closest thing I have to a cofounder. A brilliant engineer as well as a masterful corporate tactician, he possesses a unique set of skills; as chief operating officer and vice chairman, he has been and continues to be vital to the company's success. Jeff is not only a great teammate, but a great friend.

And it's important that I thank Gregg Lemkau, Marc Lisker, John Phelan, Rob Platek, and all my partners at MSD Capital and MSD Partners who are building a significant alternative asset investment firm.

But mostly I want to acknowledge my family—and especially my mother. Once I managed to persuade her out of her initial conviction that I should become a doctor (sorry about that, Mom!), she was with me every step of the way, always positive, always knowing what I needed. My father blames my success on her, which is at least half true! My parents taught my brothers and me that we could do anything; they fueled our curiosity and desire to learn. They also taught us the difference between right and wrong, and most of all, to respect all people and take care of each other. I've been very lucky to have such great parents.

I've always wanted to be a great husband and father. I was smitten when I first met Susan, and marrying her was the single best decision of my life. I love her more and more every day. She has made me a better person and inspires me in all I do. She is my best friend, my confidante, and my partner in all things. She has also lived almost every moment in this book with me and was instrumental in refining the manuscript. Together we are very proud of each of our children, Kira, Alexa, Zachary, and Juliette, who are all paving their own successful paths in the world.

And I want to thank my two brothers, Steven and Adam, who have always been there for me and whom I love very much.

As I say in the book, I am so grateful to have been born in the United

States, where I had access to great schools—and where, by great good luck, I found myself at the dawn of the microprocessor age, looking with intense curiosity toward whatever was going to come next.

I must acknowledge the brilliant Janet Mountain and the amazing team at the Michael and Susan Dell Foundation, who have brought to life our family's charitable ambitions with great results.

My deep gratitude goes to all our competitors over the years. They've been a source of abundant motivation and inspiration (to beat them), especially when they publicly doubted us. I've learned from their successes, and probably even more from their failures, which have taught me a great deal about what not to do and how not to do it.

Many thanks to my excellent literary agent, Pilar Queen, and to my superb editors Adrian Zackheim and Trish Daly, along with the whole team at Portfolio.

And last but certainly not least, I also want to acknowledge and thank our readers, and hope that this story inspires others in some way.

Appendix

THINGS I BELIEVE

The following, in no particular order, are principles, traits, ideals, and lessons that have helped me and our company succeed:

1. Curiosity. Have I mentioned curiosity already? It's so important, I'll say it again: Always be learning. You want to have big ears. To listen, to learn, and to always be curious. To be open to ambiguity. Design your company from the customer back.

2. Use facts and data to make decisions. Be objective and humble and willing to change your mind if the facts and data suggest that's what is needed. The scientific method works in business.

3. Commitment, drive, grit, determination, perseverance, indomitable will—you must have these qualities.

4. Try never to be the smartest person in the room. Surround yourself with people who challenge you, teach you, inspire you, and

push you to be your best. And learn to recognize and appreciate people's different talents.

5. Trustworthiness, ethics, and integrity are paramount. You can't be successful over time without these values. Markets are long-term efficient. If I make a commitment and don't meet it, or if I deliver a bad product or service, no one will want to buy from me again.

6. The rate of change is only increasing. It will not slow down in the future.

7. You must change or die. There are only the quick and the dead. Organizations need to constantly reimagine themselves, understanding and anticipating all the factors, including and especially technology, that will impact them in the future.

8. Ideas are a commodity. Execution of them is not. Coming up with a great idea or strategy is necessary but not sufficient for success. You must execute. This requires detailed operational discipline and understanding.

9. Teams win championships, not players. Always put the team ahead of the player.

10. Life is about taking a punch, falling down, getting back up and fighting again! (See number 3.)

11. Never let a good crisis go to waste—and if there is no crisis, create one (as a way of motivating change and progress). During a crisis—or any other time—focus on what you can control. Crises often create new opportunities. Instead of wallowing in your problems, find the opportunity.

12. Don't be a victim, ever. Victimhood is a losing mindset. Self-determination requires focusing on what you can control and drive forward.

13. Confidence, not arrogance. Humility, not ego.

14. Everybody gets angry. But don't stay angry. Anger is counterproductive. Instead, be motivated by a desire to help others and . . . Love, Family, Country, Compassion, and Mastery.

15. Be (as we like to say at Dell) pleased but never satisfied. This means improving continuously—the Japanese call it *kaizen*. It means being in a race with no finish line. Celebrate and appreciate achievements, but always look ahead to the next big goal or opportunity.

16. Success is a horrible teacher. (See numbers 3 and 10.) Setbacks and failures make you stronger over time—if you let yourself learn from them.

17. Be willing to take risks, experiment, and test things. As the rate of change increases, small experiments will build a path to success.

18. (See number 13) Humility, openness, fairness, and authenticity.

19. Have respect for others and treat them as you want to be treated.

20. Optimism . . . obviously! Finding ways to grow optimism in yourself will make you much happier.

21. Find purpose and passion in your life by being part of something greater than yourself.